Korean Folktales
in Everyday Conversation:
Must-Know Stories
for Korean Learners

일상 속에서 진짜 자주 등장하는 **한국 옛날이야기**

Korean Folktales in Everyday Conversation:
Must-Know Stories for Korean Learners

일상 속에서 진짜 자주 등장하는 **한국 옛날이야기**

1판 1쇄 · 1st edition published	2024. 1. 2.
1판 2쇄 · 2nd edition published	2024. 1. 8.

지은이 · Written by	Talk To Me In Korean
책임편집 · Edited by	선경화 Kyunghwa Sun, 석다혜 Dahye Seok, 김지나 Jina Kim
디자인 · Designed by	이은정 Eunjeong Lee
디자인 총괄 · Design directed by	선윤아 Yoona Sun
일러스트레이션 · Illustrations by	김라온 Laon Kim
녹음 · Voice Recordings by	선경화 Kyunghwa Sun, 유승완 Seungwan Yu, 석다혜 Dahye Seok
오디오 편집 · Audio Editing by	김한나 Hanna Kim, 문준배 Joonbae Moon
펴낸곳 · Published by	롱테일북스 Longtail Books
펴낸이 · Publisher	이수영 Su Young Lee
편집 · Copy-edited by	강지희 Jihee Kang
주소 · Address	04033 서울특별시 마포구 양화로 113, 3층(서교동, 순흥빌딩)
	3rd Floor, 113 Yanghwa-ro, Mapo-gu, Seoul, KOREA
이메일 · E-mail	TTMIK@longtailbooks.co.kr
ISBN	979-11-91343-60-1 13710

*이 교재의 내용을 사전 허가 없이 전재하거나 복제할 경우 법적인 제재를 받게 됨을 알려 드립니다.

*잘못된 책은 구입하신 서점이나 본사에서 교환해 드립니다.

*정가는 표지에 표시되어 있습니다.

TTMIK - TALK TO ME IN KOREAN

Korean Folktales
in Everyday Conversation:
Must-know Stories
for Korean Learners

일상 속에서 진짜 자주 등장하는
한국 옛날이야기

Contents

Preface

How often will you encounter idiomatic Korean expressions that are based on a well-known story or cultural reference? The answer is every single day.

This book is designed to help you learn such Korean expressions through stories, and expand your understanding of Korean culture at the same time. All the stories in this book are very familiar to every native Korean speaker because they grew up hearing them all the time.

Reading the folktales themselves is also going to be very entertaining; these stories are famous because they are good! But understanding the modern application of the stories, in other words, how people reference them in their day-to-day conversations, is going to be even more interesting.

일상 속에서 진짜 자주 등장하는 한국 옛날이야기

Along with a full translation for each story, key vocabulary information is also provided so that you don't have to look up every new word. In the modern application section of each chapter, you will also see easy-to-follow explanations and realistic examples of how you can form your own sentences using the key phrase from the story.

We believe that this book will make your study of the Korean language more diverse, more effective, and more enjoyable. Get ready to level-up your Korean reading and speaking skills!

How to Use This Book

놀부 심보가 따로 없다!

You're acting just like Nolbu!

This is what you might say in a situation like the one in this illustration.
Try to guess what kind of situation this is before you discover the meaning and usage of the expression on the following pages.

How come?
Find out on the next page

→

흥부와 놀부

옛날 어느 마을에 흥부와 놀부 형제가 살고 있었어요. 동생 흥부는 착했지만
많았어요.

그러던 어느 날, 흥부와 놀부
"놀부야, 흥부야, 사이좋게 지 사이좋게 지내야 한다. 재산은 꼭 둘이 나누어 가져라."
하지만 욕심쟁이 놀부는 아 놀부는 아버지의 말을 듣지 않고 재산을 모두 차지했어요. 그리고 흥부네
모두 내쫓았어요.

흥부네 가족들은 산 밑에 오두막집을 짓고 살게 되었어요. 흥부는 가족들을 위해 먹을 것을
구하려고 했지만, 겨울이라 먹을 것을 구하기가 어려웠어요.
"아버지, 배고파요."
"아버지, 집에 먹을 게 아무것도 없어요."
아무것도 먹지 못하고 있는 아이들을 보자 흥부는 마음이 아팠어요.
"안 되겠어요, 여보. 오늘은 형님 집에 찾아가 볼게요."
흥부는 어쩔 수 없이 놀부를 찾아갔어요.

> In Korean, double quotation marks are used for conversational statements, and single quotation marks are used for internal thoughts.

> The sentences highlighted in purple are explained in the Grammar Point section at the back of this book.

욕심 greed 돌아가시다 to pass away 사이좋다 to be on good terms 재산 property, wealth
욕심쟁이 disapproving/casual greedy person 차지하다 to possess, to take 내쫓다 to kick out
오두막집 shack 짓다 to build 구하다 to find 배고프다 to be hungry 여보 honey (to one's wife or
husband) 형님 honorific older brother 굶다 to starve 이놈 brat

> In the vocabulary list, you will encounter the markers "honorific" and "disapproving/casual". The words marked with "honorific" are used to show respect, while the words marked with "disapproving/casual" are used to show disrespect or casual speech.

> If you come across a new word while reading the story, you can find the English definition at the bottom of the page.
>
> Proper nouns, such as place names and titles, are romanized and italicized, provided with an explanation instead of a definition.

Heungbu and Nolbu

 Track 19

Once upon a time in a village, there lived two brothers named
Heungbu, the younger brother, was kindhearted, but Nolbu, th
greedy.

And then one day, their father passed away. Before he passe
"Nolbu and Heungbu, live in harmony and divide the inheritan
However, greedy Nolbu did not listen and took all the inherita
kicked Heungbu and his family out of their house.

Heungbu and his family built a shack at the foot of a mountain and lived there. Heungbu
tried to find food for his family, but it was difficult because it was winter.
"Father, I am hungry."
"Father, there is nothing to eat at home."
Seeing his children not being able to eat anything, Heungbu felt heartbroken.
"I cannot take it anymore, honey. Today, I will visit my brother's house."
Heungbu had no other choice but to go to Nolbu's house.

You can listen to native Korean
speakers read the stories with the
audio files.
The audio files are available
for listening on our mobile app
TTMIK: Audio or by streaming/
downloading them from our
website, https://talktomeinkorean.
com/audio.

Here are some illustrations
to give you visual context
for the stories.

Here, you can check how well you have understood the story by taking a short quiz.

○ Comprehension Quiz

Read the statements below and mark them as true or false.

1. 놀부는 욕심이 많다.   True / False
2. 흥부는 놀부의 형이다.   True / False
3. 흥부는 새끼 제비의 다리를 치료해 주었다.   True / False
4. 놀부가 박을 잘랐을 때 보물이 나왔다.   True / False
5. 흥부는 부자가 되었다.   True / False

Modern Application ○·······

In addition to providing background information about the story, this part also explains how Koreans incorporate the story into everyday conversation in modern life, with examples of dialogues provided.

"Heungbu and Nolbu" is one of the most well-known Korean
Koreans are familiar with its plot and characters.

In particular, the character "Nolbu" is most frequently mentio
casual 놀부 같다. (= The person is just like Nolbu.)", " ca
아니고. (= You're not Nolbu or something.)" when referring t
jealous, greedy, or stingy. This type of characteristic is also
"놀부 심보 (= Nolbu-like state of mind)", which can be expres
like " casual 무슨 놀부 심보야? (= What kind of Nolbu-like beha
" casual 놀부 심보가 따로 없다. (= That's exactly the kind of thing Nolbu would
do.)"

The formality of the situations in which Koreans quote the story varies. If the presented expression is mostly used in casual language within close relationships, it is written in 반말(casual language) and is marked with "casual".

Example Dialogue (1)

Track 20

도윤: 이것 좀 봐. 나 이 신발 반값에 샀다! 5만 원에 샀어.

다혜: 와, 진짜 싸다! 참, 이 신발 예지도 사고 싶다고 했는데. 예지한테도
주자.

도윤: 다른 애들한테는 말하지 마. 그럼 내가 할인받은 기분이 안 나잖아.

다혜: 뭐라고? 놀부 심보가 따로 없다, 정말.

Doyun: Look at these. I bought these shoes at half price! I got
for 50,000 won.

Dahye: Wow, that's really cheap! By the way, Yeji said she wa
to buy these shoes too. Let's tell her.

Doyun: Don't tell other people. Otherwise, I won't feel like I go
good deal.

Dahye: What? You're acting just like Nolbu, seriously.

Example Dialogue (2)

엄마: 아들, 동생한테도 과자 하나 줘야지.

아들: 싫어요! 저만 먹을 거예요!

엄마: 같이 먹으라고 사 준 건데 놀부처럼 그러면 안 되지!

Mother: Son, you should give your younger sibling a snack too.

Son: I don't want to! I'm going to eat it all by myself!

Mother: I bought it for both of you to share. You shouldn't act like
Nolbu!

You can practice conversations with audio tracks recorded by native Korean speakers.
Each conversation is played twice for you to practice listening and speaking.

Answers

1. True 2. False 3. True 4. False 5. True

You can find the answers to the Comprehension Quiz here.

Key grammar points from each story are provided in the Grammar Point section at the back of the book. We have selected important grammar points that appear more than twice in the story.

Grammar Point

01 **I Am Not Scared of Tigers!**
호랑이와 곶감 The Tiger and the Dried Persimmon

-(으)ㄴ 줄 알다

= to know/think that someone has done something; to know/think that something/someone is + descriptive verb

It's used to express your knowledge or assumption about a past action or a present state. To make this expression a negative sentence, either change 알다 to 모르다, or add 안 to the verb that comes before -(으)ㄴ 줄 알다.

Excerpt:

호랑이는 등에 곶감이라는 무서운 놈이 탄 줄 알고 힘껏 뛰기 시작했어요.

The tiger, thinking that the thief was a scary dried persimmon, started running with all its might.

호랑이도 곶감이 등에서 떨어진 줄 알고 더 빨리 뛰어 도망갔어요.

The tiger also thought that the dried persimmon had fallen off its back and ran away faster.

01

I Am Not
Scared of Tigers!

How come?
Find out on the next page

호랑이와 곶감

어느 추운 겨울 밤이었어요. 배고픈 호랑이 한 마리가 먹을 것을 찾아 마을로 내려왔어요.

"어흥. 배고파."

그때 아이 울음소리가 들렸어요.

"으앙! 으앙!"

호랑이는 소리가 나는 집을 찾기 시작했어요.

"오호! 저 집이구나!"

호랑이는 엄마와 아이가 있는 집에 도착했어요. 그리고 조용히 문 앞까지 다가갔어요.

"으앙! 으앙!"

아이는 여전히 큰 소리로 울고 있었어요.

"얘야, 그만 울어. 계속 울면 도깨비가 와서 잡아갈 거야!"

엄마의 말에 아이는 더 크게 '으앙' 하고 울었어요. 아이의 울음소리를 들은 호랑이는

생각했어요.

'도깨비를 안 무서워하네! 역시 이 호랑이 정도는 돼야 무섭지!'

곶감 dried persimmon   어흥 roar   배고프다 to be hungry   울음소리 crying sound   으앙 waaah (sound of
a baby crying)   소리가 나다 to sound   오호 aha   다가가다 to approach   여전히 still   얘 hey, kid
도깨비 goblin   잡아가다 to take away

The Tiger and the Dried Persimmon

It was a cold winter night. A hungry tiger came down to the village looking for something to eat.

"Roar. I am hungry."

Just then, it heard the sound of a child crying.

"Waaah! Waaah!"

The tiger began to search for the house where the sound was coming from.

"Aha! It is that house!"

The tiger arrived at a house where there was a mother and a child. Then, quietly, it approached the front door.

"Waaah! Waaah!"

The child was still crying loudly.

"Hey, stop crying. If you keep crying, goblins will come and take you away!"

Upon hearing the mother's words, the child cried even louder, "Waaah!" Upon hearing the sound of the child crying, the tiger thought to itself,

"This kid is not afraid of goblins! As expected, it will take a tiger to scare him!"

그때였어요. 아이 엄마가 아이에게 말했어요.

"얘야, 그만 울어. 밖에 무서운 호랑이가 와 있어. 계속 울면 호랑이가 잡아갈 거야."

'아니! 내가 여기에 있는 걸 어떻게 알았지?'

호랑이는 깜짝 놀랐어요. 그런데도 아이는 여전히 울음을 그치지 않았어요.

'저 애는 내가 무섭지도 않나 봐!'

호랑이는 당황했어요.

엄마가 아이에게 다시 말했어요.

"얘야, 엄마가 곶감 줄게. 곶감."

곶감이라는 말에 아이가 곧바로 울음을 그쳤어요. 호랑이는 생각했어요.

'곶감이라는 놈이 누구길래 이렇게 곧바로 울음을 그치지? 곶감은 나보다 더 무서운 놈이구나.'

그런데 그때, 엄마가 방문을 열었어요. 호랑이는 깜짝 놀라 외양간 안으로 도망갔어요.

외양간 안에 숨어 있던 호랑이는 누군가 외양간으로 살금살금 들어오는 것을 봤어요.

'저게 곶감이구나!'

호랑이는 생각했어요. 그런데 사실 외양간 안으로 들어온 사람은 소를 훔치러 온

소도둑이었어요. 호랑이는 그것도 모르고 무서워서 벌벌 떨었어요. 그리고 소 옆에 몸을

엎드리고 숨었어요.

울음 crying   그치다 to stop   당황하다 to be puzzled   곧바로 immediately   놈 disapproving/casual guy

외양간 barn   도망가다 to run away   살금살금 quietly   훔치다 to steal   소도둑 cattle thief

벌벌 mimetic word describing someone trembling   떨다 to tremble   엎드리다 to lie face down

숨다 to hide

It was then that the mother said to the child, "Hey, stop crying. There is a scary tiger outside. If you keep crying, the tiger will take you away."
"What? How did she know I was here?"
The tiger was startled. However, the child still did not stop crying.
"I guess this kid is not even afraid of me!"
The tiger was puzzled.

The mother spoke again to the child, "Hey, I will give you some dried persimmons. Dried persimmons."
At the mention of dried persimmons, the child immediately stopped crying. The tiger thought to itself, "Who is this 'dried persimmon' that can make the child stop crying so suddenly? Dried persimmons must be scarier than me."
At that moment, the mother opened the door, and the tiger was startled and ran into the barn.

While hiding inside the barn, the tiger saw someone sneaking into the barn quietly.
"That must be a dried persimmon!"
The tiger thought to itself. But in fact, the person who entered the barn was a cattle thief. The tiger, not knowing this, trembled in fear. Then it crouched down next to the cow and hid.

바로 그때, 천천히 다가온 소도둑이 호랑이 머리를 더듬었어요. 호랑이는 깜짝 놀라 벌떡
일어났어요. 그런데 벌떡 일어난 호랑이 때문에 소도둑이 깜짝 놀라서 호랑이 등에 올라타
버렸어요.

'아이고! 내 등에 곶감이 탔잖아!'

호랑이는 등에 곶감이라는 무서운 놈이 탄 줄 알고 힘껏 뛰기 시작했어요. 소도둑도 호랑이
등에서 떨어지지 않으려고 호랑이에게 힘껏 매달렸어요. 호랑이는 생각했어요.

'이상하다. 곶감이 왜 안 떨어지지? 정말 무서운 놈이야!'

호랑이 등에 매달려 가던 소도둑은 소가 너무 빠른 것이 이상하다고 생각했어요.

'이상하다. 소가 왜 이렇게 빠르지?'

어느새 날이 밝았어요. 그제야 소도둑은 자신이 호랑이를 타고 있다는 것을 알게 됐어요.

'세상에! 내가 지금 호랑이 등에 올라타 있잖아!'

소도둑은 너무 무서웠어요. 그런데 그때, 커다란 나무가 보였어요. 소도둑은 재빨리 뛰어서
나무에 매달렸어요. 그리고 소도둑은 호랑이를 피해 멀리 도망갔어요.

'아이고. 호랑이한테 잡아먹힐 뻔했네!'

호랑이도 곶감이 등에서 떨어진 줄 알고 더 빨리 뛰어 도망갔어요.

'아이고. 곶감한테 잡아먹힐 뻔했네!'

그 후에 호랑이와 소도둑은 다시는 마을로 오지 않았다고 해요. 호랑이는 곶감이, 소도둑은
호랑이가 너무 무서웠거든요.

다가오다 to approach, to come toward   더듬다 to fumble   벌떡 mimetic word describing someone
standing up suddenly   올라타다 to get onto   아이고 jeez   힘껏 with all one's might   매달리다 to hang
onto, to cling onto   어느새 before one knows   그제야 only then   세상에 oh my   커다랗다 to be big
재빨리 quickly   피하다 to avoid   잡아먹다 to feed on, to prey on

Just then, the cattle thief approached the tiger slowly and touched its head. The tiger was startled and jumped up. But because the tiger suddenly stood up, the thief was startled and ended up getting onto the tiger's back.

"Jeez! A dried persimmon is on my back!"

The tiger, thinking that there was a scary dried persimmon on his back, started running with all its might. The thief also held onto the tiger tightly, not wanting to fall off the tiger's back. The tiger thought to itself, "This is strange. Why won't the dried persimmon fall off? It really is a scary creature!"

Meanwhile, the thief who was riding on the tiger's back, found it strange that a cow was so fast.

"This is strange. Why is the cow so fast?"

Before they knew it, it was morning. Only then did the cattle thief realize that he was riding on a tiger.

"Oh, my! I am riding on a tiger's back right now!"

The cattle thief was very frightened. But then he saw a big tree. He quickly jumped off and clung onto the tree. Then, he ran far away to escape from the tiger.

"Jeez. I was almost eaten by a tiger!"

The tiger also thought that the dried persimmon had fallen off its back and ran away faster.

"Jeez. I was almost eaten by a dried persimmon!"

It is said that after that day, the tiger and the cattle thief did not return to the village.

It was because the tiger was very afraid of the dried persimmon,

and the cattle thief was very afraid of the tiger.

Comprehension Quiz

Read the statements below and mark them as true or false.

1. 아이는 도깨비가 잡아간다고 하니까 울음을 그쳤다. —————— True / False
2. 호랑이는 곶감을 무서워한다. ——————————————— True / False
3. 외양간에 들어온 사람은 소도둑이었다. ——————— True / False
4. 소도둑은 호랑이를 훔치기 위해 호랑이 등에 올라탔다. —— True / False
5. 소도둑은 호랑이한테 잡아먹혔다. ——————————— True / False

Modern Application

Tigers and dried persimmons are both considered to be the favorite animal and snack in Korea. Tigers often appear in Korean folktales because Korea is a mountainous country where tigers were abundant in the past. Tigers were considered the scariest animals at that time, so parents often said " casual 자꾸 울면 호랑이가 잡아간다! (= If you keep crying, a tiger will come and take you away!)", " casual 호랑이가 잡아가기 전에 뚝 그쳐! (= Stop crying before the tiger takes you away!)" to make their children stop crying.

But there was something more effective than a scary tiger: delicious dried persimmons. In the old days, before modern snacks existed, dried persimmons were among the best treats for children because they were sweet, chewy, and jelly-like. So when children were given a dried persimmon, they would stop crying quickly.

Meanwhile, Koreans regarded tigers as frightening, but also familiar and amusing creatures. In this story, the tiger is portrayed as a funny creature

running away from the dried persimmon, and this is where the expression
"호랑이도 무서워하는 곶감 (= Dried persimmons that even tigers are afraid of)"
came from.

Example Dialogue Track 02

아빠: 그만 울어. 오늘은 의사 선생님만 보는 거야.

딸: 으앙! 으앙!

아빠: 무서운 거 아니야. 울지 마.

딸: 으앙! 으앙!

아빠: 뚝! 너 자꾸 울면 호랑이가 잡아간다!

Dad: Stop Crying. Today you're only seeing the doctor.

Daughter: Waaah! Waaah!

Dad: It's not scary. Don't cry.

Daughter: Waaah! Waaah!

Dad: Shush! If you keep crying, a tiger will come and take you away!

Whatever You Say, I Will Do the Opposite

How come?
Find out on the next page

청개구리 이야기

어느 작은 연못에 엄마 청개구리와 아들 청개구리가 살고 있었어요. 아들 청개구리는 엄마 청개구리의 말을 잘 듣지 않았어요. 무엇이든지 거꾸로 행동해서 엄마 청개구리의 마음을 아프게 했어요.

"얘야, 더러운 곳에서 놀지 말렴. 깨끗한 곳에서 놀아."
엄마 청개구리가 이렇게 말하면 아들 청개구리는 지저분한 흙탕물에서 마구 헤엄치며 **놀**았어요.

"얘야, 숲속에는 뱀이 많으니까 가지 마. 위험해."
엄마 청개구리가 이렇게 말하면 아들 청개구리는 일부러 숲속에 가서 놀았어요. 하마터면 뱀한테 잡아먹힐 뻔한 적이 한두 번이 아니었어요.

"얘야, '개굴개굴' 하고 울어 보렴."
엄마 청개구리가 우는 법을 가르쳐 주었어요. 하지만 아들 청개구리는 엄마 말과 반대로, '굴개굴개' 하고 울었어요.

청개구리 tree frog, green frog 연못 pond 말을 듣다 to do as one is told 거꾸로 in reverse 애 hey, kid
지저분하다 to be dirty 흙탕물 muddy water 마구 wildly, carelessly 헤엄치다 to swim 숲속 forest
뱀 snake 일부러 deliberately 하마터면 almost 잡아먹다 to feed on, to prey on 개굴개굴 rib-bit, rib-bit
(sound that a frog makes)

The Green Frogs

In a small pond, there lived a mother frog and her son. The son frog did not listen to his mother very well. He hurt his mother's feelings by acting contrary to whatever she said.

"Hey, do not play in dirty places. Play in clean places."
If the mother frog said this, the son would play in dirty and muddy water, carelessly swimming in it.

"Hey, do not go into the forest because there are many snakes. It is dangerous."
If the mother frog said this, the son frog would deliberately go into the forest to play.
He was almost eaten by a snake more than once or twice.

"Hey, try making this sound 'gae-gul-gae-gul (rib-bit, rib-bit)'."
The mother frog taught her son how to make frog sounds. However, the son made the opposite sound "gul-gae-gul-gae".

청개구리 이야기

이렇게 아들 청개구리는 엄마의 말에 무조건 반대로 행동했어요. 엄마 청개구리는 이런 아들 청개구리 때문에 정말 속상했어요.
"어휴, 저렇게 말을 안 들어서 어떻게 하지."

그러던 어느 날, 엄마 청개구리가 큰 병에 걸렸어요. 엄마 청개구리는 자신이 곧 죽게 될 것을 알았어요. 그래서 아들 청개구리를 불러서 이렇게 말했어요.
"내가 죽으면 나를 꼭 시냇가에 묻어 주렴. 절대 산에 묻으면 안 돼."
엄마 청개구리는 산에 묻히고 싶었어요. 하지만 산에 묻어 달라고 하면 아들이 자신을 시냇가에 묻어 줄까 봐 걱정됐어요. 그래서 일부러 산이 아닌 시냇가에 묻어 달라고 했어요. 그러면 아들이 반대로 자신을 산에 묻어 줄 거라고 생각했어요.

얼마 뒤, 엄마 청개구리는 세상을 떠나고 말았어요. 엄마 청개구리가 죽자 아들 청개구리는 눈물을 펑펑 흘렸어요.
"내가 말을 듣지 않아서 엄마가 큰 병에 걸리셨던 거야. 나 때문에 엄마가 돌아가셨어. 흑흑..."
아들 청개구리는 엄마 말을 듣지 않았던 걸 후회했어요.

무조건 unconditionally, definitely   속상하다 to be upset   어휴 sound of sighing   병에 걸리다 to fall ill
시냇가 stream bank, by the stream   묻다 to bury   절대 never   세상을 떠나다 to die, to pass away
눈물을 흘리다 to shed tears   펑펑 mimetic word describing a large amount of liquid pouring at once
돌아가시다 to pass away   흑흑 sound of sobbing   후회하다 to regret

Like this, the son always did the opposite of what his mother said. The mother frog was really upset because her son behaved like this.

"Sigh, he never listens to me. What am I to do with him?"

And then one day, the mother frog fell ill with a serious illness and knew that she would die soon. She called her son and said, "When I die, make sure to bury me near the stream. Never bury me in the mountains."

The mother frog wanted to be buried in the mountains. However, she was worried that her son would bury her near the stream if she asked him to bury her in the mountains. So, she deliberately asked to be buried near the stream, thinking that her son would bury her in the mountains instead.

Some time later, the mother frog passed away. When the mother frog died, the son burst into tears.

"My mom got seriously ill because I did not listen to her. Mom passed away because of me. (Sob...)"

The son regretted not having listened to his mother.

그리고 아들 청개구리는 이렇게 생각했어요.
'마지막으로 엄마가 남기신 말씀은 꼭 들어야지.'
아들 청개구리는 엄마 청개구리가 말한 그대로 엄마 청개구리를 시냇가에 묻었어요.

엄마를 묻은 후, 하루는 비가 많이 내리기 시작했어요. 아들 청개구리는 갑자기 엄마
청개구리의 무덤이 걱정되기 시작했어요.
'비가 와서 엄마 무덤이 떠내려가면 어떡하지? 안 되겠다. 내가 가서 무덤을 지켜야겠어.'
시냇가에 가서 보니 엄마 청개구리의 무덤이 정말로 떠내려가려고 했어요. 아들 청개구리는
무덤이 떠내려갈까 봐 걱정돼 크게 소리 내어 울었어요.

그날 이후, 아들 청개구리는 비가 오는 날이면 엄마 청개구리의 무덤으로 갔어요. 그리고
'개굴개굴' 하고 울면서 무덤을 지켰어요. 그래서 지금도 비가 오는 날이면 시냇가에 있는
청개구리가 '개굴개굴' 하고 크게 우는 거라고 해요.

무덤 grave   떠내려가다 to be washed away   정말로 really

And then the son frog thought to himself, "I must obey the final words that Mom left behind."

The son frog buried his mother just as his mother had asked, by the stream.

After burying his mother, it started to rain heavily one day. The son suddenly became worried about his mother's grave.

"What if the grave gets washed away by the rain? I cannot let that happen. I have to go and protect the grave."

When he went to the stream to check, his mother's grave was really about to be washed away. The son was worried that the grave might be washed away and cried out loud.

Since that day, whenever it rained, the son frog went to his mom's grave and cried out, "rib-bit, rib-bit", while guarding the grave. That is why even now, on rainy days, the frogs by the stream loudly cry out "rib-bit, rib-bit."

Comprehension Quiz

Read the statements below and mark them as true or false.

1. 아들 청개구리는 엄마의 말을 잘 듣지 않았다. ⸻ True / False
2. 엄마 청개구리는 아들에게 숲속에서 놀라고 했다. ⸻ True / False
3. 엄마 청개구리는 시냇가에 묻히고 싶었다. ⸻ True / False
4. 엄마 청개구리의 무덤이 떠내려갔다. ⸻ True / False
5. 아들 청개구리는 비가 오는 날마다 시냇가에서 크게 운다. ⸻ True / False

Modern Application

In this story, the son frog does the opposite of what his mother says to do. So, people who are disobedient, or who do more of what they are told not to do are often called "청개구리 (= tree frog, green frog)". This is why it's frequently used to describe children who don't listen to their parents, but it can also be used regardless of age. You can use it in phrases like " casual 청개구리처럼 왜 그래? (= Why are you acting like a green frog?)", " casual 청개구리같이 굴지 마. (= Don't behave like a green frog.)" It's also used as a proverb " casual 말 안 듣기는 청개구리 같다. (= You're being stubborn like a green frog.)", which originated from this story.

Example Dialogue

(Track 04)

연우: 어디 나가려고? 몸도 안 좋은데, 집에서 쉬지.

진호: 너무 답답해서.

연우: 평소에는 나가라고 해도 안 나가면서. 청개구리같이 왜 그래?

진호: 나가지 말라고 하니까 더 나가고 싶어. 나 진짜 청개구리 같다.

Yeonu: Are you going out somewhere? You're not feeling well, so you should rest at home.

Jinho: I feel too frustrated.

Yeonu: Usually, even if I tell you to go out, you don't go. Why are you acting like a green frog?

Jinho: Since you're telling me not to go out, I want to go out even more. I really am like a green frog.

03

Darkness Cannot Stop Us

How come?
Find out on the next page

한석봉과 어머니

어느 작은 마을에 한석봉이라는 아이가 있었어요. 석봉의 아버지는 일찍 돌아가셔서 석봉은
어머니와 둘이서 살았어요. 석봉의 어머니는 떡을 만들어서 시장에 파는 일을 했어요. 석봉은
어릴 때부터 글자에 관심이 많았어요.

"어머니, 이 글자는 어떻게 읽어요?"

"'나무'라고 읽지."

"그럼 이거는요?"

"그건 '하늘'이야."

"너무 재미있어요! 글자가 꼭 예쁜 그림 같아요."

어머니가 시장에서 일을 하시는 동안 한석봉은 서당에 가지 않는 친구들과 놀았어요. 석봉의
친구들은 매일 밖에서 노는 것을 좋아했지만, 석봉은 친구들과 노는 것이 점점 지루해졌어요.

"어머니, 저도 서당에 다니고 싶어요. 그리고 글자를 배우고 싶어요."

어머니는 마음이 아팠어요. 석봉의 집은 아주 가난해서 서당에 다닐 수 없었거든요.

"글자를 왜 배우고 싶니?"

"글자를 배워서 예쁜 글씨를 쓰고 싶어요. 화가처럼요."

돌아가시다 to pass away   떡 rice cake   글자 letter   지루하다 to be boring/bored   서당 elementary
school during the Joseon Dynasty   가난하다 to be poor   글씨 handwriting, calligraphy   화가 painter

Han Seokbong and His Mother

There was a child called Han Seokbong in a small village. His father passed away at an early age, so he lived with only his mother. His mother made rice cakes and sold them at the market. He was very interested in letters from a young age.

"Mother, how do you read this letter?"

"It says 'na-mu (tree)'."

"Then how about this one?"

"That is 'ha-neul (sky)'."

"This is so much fun! The letters really look like pretty drawings."

While his mother was working at the market, Han Seokbong hung out with his friends who did not go to school. His friends liked to hang out outside every day, but he was gradually getting bored of hanging out with his friends.

"Mother, I want to go to school, too. Also, I want to learn to read and write."

His mother was heart-broken because Seokbong's family was so poor that he could not go to school.

"Why do you want to learn letters?"

"I want to learn letters and write them in pretty calligraphy, like a painter."

한석봉과 어머니

석봉의 대답을 듣고 어머니는 이렇게 말했어요.

"엄마가 서당은 보내 줄 수 없지만, 우리 석봉이가 글씨 연습을 할 수 있는 종이는 꼭 사 줄게."

석봉은 실망했어요. 하지만 어머니가 힘들게 일하는 걸 알고 있어서 더 이야기하지 않았어요.

석봉은 매일 서당에 가서 다른 아이들이 공부하는 것을 구경했어요. 그리고 집에 돌아와서

나뭇가지로 서당에서 본 글자들을 따라 썼어요.

한 달 뒤, 석봉의 생일이었어요. 어머니가 종이와 붓을 사 오셨어요.

"석봉아, 이거 갖고 싶었지? 생일 축하한다."

"와! 어머니, 이건 종이잖아요? 너무 행복해요! 감사합니다!"

한석봉은 종이와 붓을 가진 것만으로도 너무 기뻤어요. 어머니는 그런 석봉을 보고

흐뭇해했어요. 석봉은 처음으로 종이 위에 글자를 써 봤어요. 종이에 글씨를 쓰는 느낌이 정말

좋아서 기분이 날아갈 것 같았어요. 글자를 쓸수록 공부하고 싶은 마음이 더 커졌어요.

"어머니, 저는 글자가 너무 좋습니다. 더 제대로 배워 보고 싶어요."

"제대로 배우려면 한양으로 가서 적어도 10년 동안은 글자 공부를 해야 해. 그래도 괜찮겠니?"

"한양이요? 그러면... 어머니와 떨어져서 살아야 하는 거예요?"

"그럼. 그 정도 각오는 해야지. 글씨로 크게 성공하려면 큰 도시에 가야 하는 거야."

"그렇지만..."

종이 paper 실망하다 to be disappointed 나뭇가지 tree branch 따라 쓰다 to trace (letters), to copy (words) 붓 brush 와 wow 흐뭇하다 to be pleased 제대로 properly 한양 *Hanyang*, the name of Seoul during the Joseon Dynasty 각오 determination

After listening to Seokbong's answer, his mother said, "Your mother (I) cannot send you to school, but for you, my Seokbong, I will definitely buy some paper to practice calligraphy on."

He was disappointed. However, he knew his mother was working hard, so he did not say anything more. He went to the school every day and watched other children study. After he got back home, he used a tree branch to try copying the letters he saw at the school.

A month later, it was Seokbong's birthday. His mother bought some paper and a brush for him.

"Seokbong, you wanted these, right? Happy birthday!"

"Wow! Mother, this is paper! I am so happy! Thank you!"

He was delighted even just to have some paper and a brush. His mother was pleased to see him like that. He wrote letters on paper for the first time. It felt so good to write letters that he felt like he could fly. The more he wrote letters, the more he wanted to study.

"Mother, I love letters. I want to learn more properly."

"If you want to learn properly, you have to go to *Hanyang* and study letters for at least 10 years. Will it still be fine?"

"Hanyang? Then... do I have to live away from you?"

"Of course. You have to have that much determination at least. You have to go to a big city in order to be highly successful through calligraphy."

"But..."

한석봉의 어머니는 단호했어요. 어머니도 아들과 떨어지는 것이 무척 슬펐지만, 한양에 보내는 것이 아들을 위한 일이라고 생각했어요. 그렇게 석봉은 한양으로 떠났어요.

한석봉의 어머니는 열심히 떡을 팔아서 한양에 있는 석봉이 공부에만 집중할 수 있도록 돈을 보내 줬어요. 석봉은 고생하시는 어머니를 위해 열심히 글씨 연습을 했어요. 그리고 3년쯤 지나자, 많은 사람들이 한석봉의 글씨를 칭찬하기 시작했어요.

"이 글씨 좀 봐. 정말 멋지다, 멋져!"

"글씨 덕분에 글의 내용이 더 좋아 보이는 것 같지 않아요?"

"그러게 말이에요. 이걸 도대체 누가 쓴 거래요?"

"한석봉이라는 청년이래요. 정말 대단하네요."

한석봉의 이름은 점점 유명해졌고, 석봉은 글씨를 써 주고 돈도 벌게 됐어요. 석봉은 이제 어머니가 계시는 집으로 돌아가도 되겠다고 생각했어요.

다음 날 아침, 석봉은 고향으로 떠났어요. 고향에 도착하니까 밤이 되었어요.

"어머니! 제가 왔어요! 어머니, 보고 싶었어요."

"뭐? 석봉이니? 떠난 지 3년밖에 안 됐는데 왜 벌써 왔어?"

어머니도 그동안 아들이 정말 보고 싶었지만 꾹 참고 단호하게 말했어요.

단호하다 to be adamant, to be firm   무척 very   집중하다 to concentrate   고생하다 to go through a hardship   도대체 (who/what/where) on earth   꾹 mimetic word describing the action of holding back or pressing something hard

Han Seokbong's mother was adamant. She was also very sad to be separated from her son, but she thought that sending him to Hanyang would be good for him. In this way, he left for Hanyang.

She worked hard selling rice cakes and sent him money so that he could only concentrate on studying in Hanyang. Seokbong, for the sake of his mother who was working hard, diligently practiced calligraphy. About three years passed, and a lot of people started to praise his calligraphy.

"Look at this calligraphy. It is really awesome! It is great!"

"Don't you feel like the calligraphy makes the content of the writing better?"

"I know, right? Who on earth wrote this?"

"I heard that it is a young man called Han Seokbong. He is really amazing."

The name, Han Seokbong, became more and more famous, and he ended up getting paid for writing letters. He thought that it was now okay to go back home where his mother was.

The next morning, Seokbong left for his hometown. By the time he arrived in his hometown, it was night.

"Mother! I am home! Mother, I missed you."

"What? Is that you, Seokbong? It has only been three years since you left. Why did you come back already?"

His mother also missed him very much over the years, but she held her feelings back and spoke sternly.

한석봉은 어머니가 반기지 않아서 당황했어요.

"어, 어머니, 제가 일찍 돌아와서 좋지 않으세요? 제 글씨 실력에 모든 사람들이 놀란다니까요! 제 이름이 한양에서 얼마나 유명한데요."

"그래? 좋다. 어서 들어오렴."

어머니는 석봉을 앉히고, 종이와 붓, 그리고 떡과 칼을 준비했어요. 그리고 방의 불을 껐어요.

"어머니, 왜 이러세요? 갑자기 왜 불을 끄시는 거예요?"

한석봉은 당황했어요.

"모두가 칭찬한다는 네 글씨를 보고 싶구나."

"그런데 불을 끄면 하나도 안 보이는데요..."

"네가 정말로 글씨를 잘 쓴다면 이렇게 어두운 곳에서도 완벽하게 쓸 수 있겠지. 나는 내일 시장에서 팔 떡을 썰 테니, 너는 글씨를 써라."

어머니는 단호하게 말했어요. 한석봉은 자신이 없었지만, 열심히 글씨를 썼어요.

10분 뒤, 어머니가 다시 불을 켰어요.

"어디 한번 볼까?"

불을 켜고 보니, 한석봉의 글씨는 삐뚤빼뚤 엉망이었어요. 하지만 어머니가 썬 떡은 두께도 똑같고 모양도 아주 예뻤어요.

"이런 글씨를 가지고 명필이라고 했니? 어서 다시 한양으로 돌아가라."

반기다 to welcome   당황하다 to be puzzled   실력 skills, ability   정말로 really   완벽하다 to be perfect
자신이 없다 to be not confident   삐뚤빼뚤 uneven   엉망 mess   두께 thickness   모양 shape
명필 masterful calligraphy, master calligrapher

일상 속에서 진짜 자주 등장하는 한국 옛날이야기

He was puzzled because his mother did not welcome him happily.

"Ah, mother, are you not happy because I came back early? Everyone is amazed by my calligraphy skills! My name is really well-known in Hanyang."

"Is that right? Good. Come on in."

Seokbong's mother had him sit down and set out paper, a brush, rice cakes, and a knife. And then she turned off the lights in the room.

"Mother, why are you doing this? Why are you turning off the lights all of a sudden?"
He was puzzled.

"I would like to see your calligraphy that you said people praise."

"But if you turn off the lights, I cannot see anything..."

"If you are really good at calligraphy, you will be able to write letters perfectly in a dark place like this. I am going to slice the rice cakes that I will sell at the market tomorrow, so you write letters."

His mother spoke sternly. He was not confident, but he tried hard to write.

10 minutes later, his mother turned the lights back on.

"Shall we have a look?"

When she looked at his letters with the lights on, they were uneven and messy. However, the rice cakes that she sliced all had the same thickness and were beautifully shaped.

"You call this kind of calligraphy masterful calligraphy? Hurry and go back to Hanyang."

어머니는 정말 마음이 아팠지만, 아들을 위해서는 단호하게 해야 한다고 생각했어요. 한석봉은 많이 슬펐지만, 자신이 쓴 글씨를 보고 아무 말도 할 수 없었어요. 석봉은 눈물을 흘리면서 한양으로 돌아갔어요.

'내가 너무 자만했어. 이렇게 부족한데 말이야. 더 열심히 해서 꼭 어머니를 기쁘게 해 드릴 거야.'

한양으로 돌아간 후 석봉은 잠도 줄이고 놀지도 않으면서 공부에만 매달렸어요. 언제 어떤 상황에서도 글씨를 잘 쓸 수 있도록 최선을 다해 연습했어요. 그렇게 7년을 더 연습한 결과, 석봉은 조선에서 그 누구보다 글씨를 잘 쓰는 사람이 되었어요. 모든 사람들이 한석봉의 글씨를 칭찬했고, 다른 나라에서 한석봉이 쓴 글씨를 비싸게 사기도 했어요.

"글씨가 정말 아름답고 멋지네요!"
"소문대로 정말 최고의 명필이 맞네요."

한석봉은 마침내 고향으로 돌아갔어요. 고향에 돌아온 석봉을 본 어머니는 무척 기뻤어요. 어머니는 석봉을 꼭 안아 주면서 말했어요.

"석봉아, 우리 아들 석봉아, 정말 장하다!"
"어머니, 그동안 고생하셨어요. 제가 이제 어머니를 행복하게 해 드릴게요."
두 모자는 눈물을 흘리면서 서로를 껴안았어요.

눈물을 흘리다 to shed tears 자만하다 to be conceited 매달리다 to be preoccupied with
최선을 다하다 to do one's best 조선 *Joseon*, the name of Korea from 1392 to 1910 소문 rumor
마침내 finally 꼭 tightly, firmly 장하다 to be admirable 껴안다 to hug

His mother felt really bad, but she thought she had to be firm for the sake of her son. He was very sad, but he could not say anything after looking at what he had written. He went back to Hanyang in tears.

"I was too conceited even though I had such poor skills. I will try harder and make my mother happy for sure."

After Seokbong went back to Hanyang, he slept less, did not play, and was preoccupied only with studying. He practiced as hard as he could so that he could write well at any time, in any situation. As a result of practicing like that for seven more years, he became the person who was better at calligraphy than anyone in all of *Joseon*. Everyone praised his calligraphy, and people from other countries also bought his calligraphy at a high price.

"The calligraphy is really beautiful and awesome!"

"He is really the best master calligrapher as the rumors say."

Han Seokbong finally went back to his hometown. His mother was very happy to see him back in their hometown. She hugged him tightly and said, "Seokbong, my son, Seokbong, I am really proud of you!"

"Mother, you have endured so much. I will make you happy from now on."

The two of them hugged each other in tears.

Comprehension Quiz

Read the statements below and mark them as true or false.

1. 한석봉은 서당에 가는 것을 싫어했다. ⸺⸺⸺⸺ True / False

2. 한석봉의 집은 가난했다. ⸺⸺⸺⸺⸺⸺ True / False

3. 한석봉의 어머니는 시장에서 옷을 팔았다. ⸺⸺ True / False

4. 한석봉은 집을 떠난 지 3년 만에 집으로 돌아왔다. ⸺ True / False

5. 한석봉이 처음 돌아왔을 때 어머니는 기뻐했다. ⸺ True / False

Modern Application

Han Seokbong is well known for his beautiful calligraphy style and his mother's resolute discipline for her son's success. The part where she said " casual 나는 떡을 썰 테니 너는 글씨를 써라. (= I am going to slice the rice cakes, so you write letters.)" is especially famous.

So, you can simply say "한석봉 글씨 같아요. (= It's like Han Seokbong's calligraphy.)" or " casual 완전 한석봉이네. (= You're really like Han Seokbong.)" to someone whose handwriting is beautiful and neat. It can also be applied as "한석봉 스타일 (= Han Seokbong's way)", when you do something in the dark. You can also say this when someone has a similar hairstyle to that of Seokbong. His hairstyle, a low braided ponytail with hair parted in the middle, is also famous.

민지: 편지 고마워. 나 진짜 감동했잖아.

제이슨: 다행이야. 한국어로 편지 쓰는 거 처음이었거든...

민지: 진짜? 글씨가 완전 한석봉이었는데? 너무 예쁘게 잘 썼어!

Minji: Thanks for the letter. I was really touched.

Jason: Good to hear. That was my first time writing a letter in Korean.

Minji: Really? Your handwriting was completely like Han Seokbong's!
You wrote it so well!

Example Dialogue (2)

(야외에서 캠핑 중)

현우: 조명 좀 줘 봐. 어두워서 고기를 못 굽겠어.

은정: 까먹고 안 가져왔는데... 어쩔 수 없지. 한석봉 스타일로 구워 보자고.

(While camping)

Hyunwoo: Give me the light. I can't grill the meat because it's too dark.

Eunjeong: I forgot to bring it. There's nothing we can do. Let's grill
the meat the Han Seokbong way.

Answers

1. False 2. True 3. False 4. True 5. False

04

Magpies
Never Forget

How come?
Find out on the next page

→

은혜 갚은 까치

옛날에 활을 잘 쏘는 한 남자가 있었어요. 어느 날, 그 남자는 한양으로 과거 시험을 보러 가고 있었어요. 남자는 한양에서 멀리 떨어진 마을에 살았어요. 그래서 시험을 보기 위해서 며칠을 걸어가야 했어요.

남자가 열심히 걷고 있을 때, 한 까치 부부가 남자의 머리 위로 날아와서 시끄럽게 울기 시작했어요. 도와달라고 하는 것 같았어요. 남자가 까치 부부 쪽을 바라보니, 커다란 뱀이 까치 둥지로 슬금슬금 기어가고 있었어요. 까치 둥지에는 새끼 까치들이 있었어요. 새끼 까치들은 겁에 질려 울고 있었어요.

"이런! 뱀이 있었구나!"

남자는 서둘러 뱀을 향해 활을 쏘았어요. 활에 정확하게 맞은 뱀은 땅에 떨어져 죽었어요. 까치 부부는 남자의 머리 위에서 한참을 돌며 고맙다고 인사했어요. 새끼 까치들을 구해 준 남자는 다시 한양을 향해 걷기 시작했어요.

한참을 걷자 주위가 어두워졌어요.

'오늘은 여기 어딘가에서 자고 가야겠구나.'

잘 곳이 있는지 주위를 둘러보니 저 멀리서 불빛이 보였어요. 남자가 불빛을 향해 다가가니 오래된 집이 하나 나타났어요.

은혜를 갚다 to repay a favor 까치 magpie 활 bow 쏘다 to shoot 한양 *Hanyang*, the name of Seoul during the Joseon Dynasty 과거 시험 the national civil service examinations under the Goryeo and Joseon Dynasties 날아오다 to fly over here 커다랗다 to be large 뱀 snake 둥지 nest 슬금슬금 stealthily, slowly 기어가다 to crawl 겁에 질리다 to be in fear 서두르다 to rush 한참 a long while 구하다 to save 둘러보다 to look around 불빛 light 향하다 to face 다가가다 to approach, to go toward

The Magpie Which Repaid a Favor

Once upon a time, there was a man who was good at shooting arrows. One day, he was on his way to take the civil service exam in *Hanyang*. The man lived in a village far away from Hanyang, so he had to walk for several days to take the exam.

While the man was walking briskly, a magpie couple flew over his head and began to make a loud noise. It seemed like they were asking for help. When the man looked in the direction of the magpie couple, he saw a large snake slithering towards the magpie nest. There were baby magpies in the nest, and they were crying in fear.
"Oh no! There is a snake!"
The man quickly shot an arrow towards the snake. The snake that was shot accurately with the arrow fell to the ground and died. The magpie couple expressed their gratitude, circling above the man's head for a long while. The man, who saved the baby magpies, began walking towards Hanyang again.

After walking for a while, the surroundings became dark.
"I guess I have to find a place to sleep around here tonight."
When he looked around for a place to sleep, he saw a light in the distance. As he approached the light, an old house appeared.

"여기 아무도 안 계세요?"

남자는 문을 두드리며 물었어요.

"누구세요?"

집에서 한 여자가 나왔어요.

"과거 시험을 보러 한양에 가는 중입니다. 죄송하지만 오늘 밤 댁에서 하루만 자고 갈 수 있을까요? 이 근처에 집이 여기 하나뿐이어서요."

"그럼요. 들어오세요."

여자는 남자에게 방도 빌려주고, 저녁밥도 차려 주었어요.

"정말 고맙습니다. 늦은 밤에 죄송해요."

"아니에요. 편하게 쉬다가 가세요."

먼 길을 걷느라 피곤했던 남자는 저녁밥을 먹자마자 잠이 들었어요.

조금 후, 잠을 자고 있던 남자는 갑자기 숨이 막혀서 눈을 떴어요. 커다란 뱀 한 마리가 남자의 몸을 감고 있었어요. 남자가 활을 쏴서 죽인 뱀만큼 아주 큰 뱀이었어요. 뱀이 남자에게 말했어요.

"네가 오늘 죽인 뱀이 내 남편이다. 내가 오늘 널 꼭 죽일 거야."

알고 보니 그 뱀은 남자가 죽인 뱀의 부인이었고, 자신의 남편을 죽인 남자에게 복수하려고 사람으로 변신했던 거였어요. 남자는 살려 달라고 간절히 말했어요.

"정말 미안해요. 하지만 당신 남편은 새끼 까치들을 잡아먹으려고 했어요. 그걸 가만히 보고 있을 수 없었어요. 용서해 주세요."

두드리다 to knock   저녁밥 dinner   차리다 to set (the table)   잠이 들다 to fall asleep
숨이 막히다 to suffocate   감다 to wind, to twine   복수하다 to avenge, to get one's revenge
변신하다 to transform   간절히 sincerely   잡아먹다 to feed on, to prey on   가만히 doing nothing, staying
still   용서하다 to forgive

"Is anyone here?"

The man asked as he knocked on the door.

"Who is it?"

A woman came out of the house.

"I am on my way to take the civil service exam in Hanyang. I am sorry, but could I stay here for just one night and leave tomorrow? This is the only house around here."

"Sure, come in."

The woman lent him a room and cooked him dinner.

"Thank you so much. I am sorry for coming so late at night."

"No problem, make yourself comfortable."

The man, who was tired from walking a long way, fell asleep right after eating dinner.

A little later, the man, who was sleeping, suddenly woke up suffocating. A large snake was wrapped around his body. It was as big as the snake he had shot and killed with his arrow earlier. The snake spoke to him.

"The snake you killed today was my husband. I will definitely kill you today."

It turned out that the snake was the wife of the snake he had killed, who had transformed into a human to seek revenge on the man who killed her husband. The man pleaded with her to spare his life.

"I am really sorry. But your husband was trying to eat the baby magpies. I could not just stand there and watch. Please forgive me."

그러자 뱀이 잠시 생각하더니 말했어요.

"저 산 위에 절이 하나 있다. 그리고 그 안에 큰 종이 있지. 아침이 되기 전에 그 종이 세 번 울리면 살려 주겠다."

"그 절은 아무도 가지 않는 절이잖아요. 이 새벽에 누가 그 절에 가서 종을 친다는 거예요? 제발 살려 주세요."

남자는 자신이 죽을 거라고 생각하고 눈물을 흘렸어요.

그런데 그때, 종소리가 들려왔어요.

"댕."

깜짝 놀란 남자와 뱀이 산을 바라보았어요. 또 종소리가 울렸어요.

"댕."

그리고 얼마 후 또다시 종소리가 '댕' 하고 울렸어요. 세 번째 종소리가 '댕' 하고 울리자, 뱀은 어쩔 수 없이 남자를 풀어 줬어요.

"약속은 약속이니까 이번에는 그냥 가지만, 다음에 꼭 다시 복수할 거야."

아침이 되었어요. 남자는 새벽에 종소리가 어떻게 났는지 궁금해서 산꼭대기의 절을 찾아갔어요. 그곳에서 남자는 죽은 까치 부부를 발견했어요. 까치 부부가 자신들의 새끼를 구해 준 남자에게 은혜를 갚기 위해 몸을 부딪쳐 종을 울렸던 거예요.

"정말 고마워. 너희가 나를 구했구나."

남자는 너무 고맙고 미안해서 눈물을 흘렸어요. 그리고 남자는 다시 한양으로 떠나기 전, 까치 부부를 잘 묻어 주었어요.

절 temple   종 bell   울리다 to ring   눈물을 흘리다 to shed tears   종소리 sound of a bell

들려오다 to sound, to reach one's ears   댕 dong, sound of a large bell ringing   또다시 once again

산꼭대기 mountaintop   발견하다 to find   부딪치다 to crash   묻다 to bury

Then the snake thought for a moment and said, "There is a temple on top of that mountain, and inside there is a big bell. If the bell rings three times before morning, I will let you live."

"But that temple is abandoned. Who would go there in the middle of the night to ring the bell? Please spare my life!"

The man shed tears, thinking that he was going to die.

But then they heard the sound of the bell ringing, "Dong."

The man and the snake were startled and looked up at the mountain. The bell rang again, "Dong."

And after a while, it rang again, "Dong." When the third ring sounded, the snake had no choice but to release the man.

"A deal is a deal, so I will let you go this time, but I will definitely get my revenge next time."

Morning came, and the man, curious about how the bell rang at the break of day, went to the temple on top of the mountain. There, he found the dead bodies of the magpie couple. The magpies had crashed into the bell to ring it in order to repay the man who had saved their babies.

"Thank you so much. You saved me."

The man cried, feeling grateful and sorry. Before he left for Hanyang again, he carefully buried the magpie couple.

Comprehension Quiz

Read the statements below and mark them as true or false.

1. 남자는 한양에 갔다가 집에 오는 중이다. ————— True / False

2. 남자는 활로 새끼 까치들을 구해 주었다. ————— True / False

3. 여자는 사람으로 변신한 뱀이었다. ————— True / False

4. 뱀은 종이 세 번 울리면 남자를 살려 주겠다고 했다. ————— True / False

5. 새끼 까치들이 종을 울렸다. ————— True / False

Modern Application

In Korea, magpies are commonly featured in traditional folktales, songs, and paintings, with a positive impression. In this story, a magpie couple even sacrificed themselves to save the person who saved their babies. The moral of the story is that even non-speaking animals repay favors, and so should humans.

Koreans often describe a person who repays a favor as "은혜 갚은 까치 (a magpie who repaid a favor)". When someone unexpectedly returns the favor you have provided, you say " casual 은혜 갚은 까치 같다. (= You're like a grateful magpie.)" or " casual 네가 무슨 은혜 갚은 까치야? (= Are you a grateful magpie or something?)".

Example Dialogue   🎧 Track 08

준우: 다혜야, 이거 너 가져.

다혜: 뭐야? 선물이야?

준우: 응. 지난번에 네가 내 과제 도와줬잖아. 은혜 갚아야지.

다혜: 와, 은혜 갚은 까치야, 뭐야? 고마워!

Junu: Dahye, take this.

Dahye: What is it? Is it a gift?

Junu: Yeah. You helped me with my assignment last time.
      I should repay the favor.

Dahye: Wow, are you a grateful magpie or what? Thank you!

05

Or Else I Will Eat You

How come?

Find out on the next page

→

해와 달이 된 남매

옛날 어느 산골 마을에 어머니와 어린 남매가 살고 있었어요. 남매의 어머니는 떡을 파는 일을 했어요.

하루는 어머니가 옆 마을에 떡을 팔러 갔다가 밤늦게 집에 돌아오고 있었어요.

"우리 애들이 기다릴 텐데... 빨리 가야겠다."

그때였어요. 커다랗고 무서운 호랑이 한 마리가 어머니 앞에 나타났어요.

"어흥! 떡 하나 주면 안 잡아먹지!"

어머니는 너무 무서웠어요. 그래서 얼른 남은 떡을 꺼내 호랑이에게 주었어요. 호랑이는 떡을 한입에 다 먹은 다음, 이렇게 말했어요.

"어흥! 떡 하나 더 주면 진짜로 안 잡아먹지!"

어머니에게는 이제 남은 떡이 없었어요.

"남은 떡이 없어요. 우리 아이들이 집에서 저를 기다리고 있어요. 제발 살려 주세요."

하지만 호랑이는 그 자리에서 어머니를 잡아먹어 버렸어요.

어머니를 잡아먹은 호랑이는 집에 아이들이 있다는 어머니의 말이 생각났어요. 호랑이는 어머니의 옷을 입었어요. 그리고 남매가 있는 집으로 갔어요.

남매 brother and sister, son and daughter 산골 mountain, mountain valley 떡 rice cake
밤늦다 to be late at night 커다랗다 to be big 어흥 roar 잡아먹다 to feed on, to prey on 얼른 quickly
한입 one bite 살리다 to spare one's life

The Brother and Sister Who Became the Sun and the Moon

Once upon a time in a mountain village, there lived a mother and her two young children, a boy and a girl. The mother sold rice cakes for a living.

One day, she went to a nearby village to sell her rice cakes and was returning home late at night.
"My children must be waiting for me... I need to hurry."
That was when a big and scary tiger appeared in front of her.
"Roar! If you give me one rice cake, I will not eat you!"
The mother was really scared. So she quickly took out the remaining rice cake and gave it to the tiger. After eating the rice cake in one bite, the tiger said, "Roar! If you give me one more rice cake, I really will not eat you!"
The mother did not have any more rice cakes left.
"I do not have any more rice cakes left. My children are waiting for me at home. Please spare my life."
However, the tiger devoured her right there and then.

After eating the mother, the tiger remembered her saying that she had children at home. The tiger then put on the mother's clothes and went to the house where the children were.

남매는 집에서 어머니가 오시기만을 기다리고 있었어요.

"엄마는 언제 오실까?"

"이제 곧 오실 거야."

그때, 누군가 문을 두드렸어요.

"얘들아, 엄마 왔다. 문 좀 열어 보렴."

"엄마!"

여동생이 문을 열려고 했어요. 그런데 그때 엄마 목소리가 이상하다는 걸 느낀 오빠가 동생을 막으며 말했어요.

"잠시만! 우리 엄마 목소리가 아니야."

호랑이는 당황했어요.

"엄마 맞아. 일을 너무 많이 해서 목소리가 쉰 거야. 어서 문 열어."

"그럼 손을 한번 내밀어 보세요."

오빠의 말에 호랑이가 문틈으로 손을 내밀었어요. 어머니의 하얀 손이 아닌 거친 털이 나 있는 손이었어요. 깜짝 놀란 오빠는 문틈으로 밖을 엿보았어요.

"세상에. 호랑이잖아! 얼른 도망가자."

문밖에 있는 호랑이를 보고 깜짝 놀란 남매는 뒷문을 통해 도망갔어요. 남매는 뒷마당에 있는 나무 위로 올라갔어요. 뒤늦게 방에 들어온 호랑이는 뒷문이 열려 있는 걸 발견했어요. 호랑이도 뒷문을 통해 밖으로 나갔어요. 호랑이는 남매를 찾기 시작했어요.

두드리다 to knock   막다 to stop   당황하다 to be flustered   쉬다 to be hoarse   내밀다 to stick out,
to reach out   문틈 a crevice or gap in the door   거칠다 to be rough   털 fur   엿보다 to peek
세상에 oh my   도망가다 to run away   문밖 outside the door   뒷문 back door   통하다 to pass through
뒷마당 backyard   뒤늦다 to be late   발견하다 to find

The siblings were eagerly waiting at home for their mother to come.

"When will Mom come?"

"She will be here soon."

Then someone knocked on the door.

"Hey kids, Mom is here. Open the door."

"Mom!"

The younger sister was going to open the door, but the older brother felt something was strange about their mom's voice and stopped her, saying:

"Just a moment! That is not our mom's voice."

The tiger was flustered.

"It is me, your mom. I have been working so much that my voice is hoarse. Hurry and open the door."

"Then stick your hand out for a moment."

At the older brother's request, the tiger pushed its hand through a gap in the door. Instead of their mother's white hand, the hand was covered in rough fur. The older brother, who was startled, peeked outside through a gap in the door.

"Oh my, it is a tiger! Quick! Let us run away!"

The siblings were startled to see the tiger outside the door and ran away through the back door. They climbed up a tree in the backyard. The tiger entered the room later, and found that the back door was open. The tiger also went outside through the back door and started to look for the siblings.

"얘들아, 어디 있니?"

뒷마당에 있는 우물에 남매의 모습이 비쳤어요. 호랑이는 우물 안에 남매가 있는 줄 알고 우물에 들어가려고 했어요.

바로 그때였어요. 나무에서 나뭇잎이 떨어져 우물 안으로 들어갔어요. 그러자 우물 안에 비친 남매의 모습이 사라졌어요. 호랑이는 남매가 우물 안에 있는 게 아니라는 걸 알게 됐어요.
"어흥! 우물 안에 숨은 게 아니었구나!"

호랑이는 나무 위에 있는 남매를 찾았어요. 그리고 남매를 따라서 나무 위로 올라가기 시작했어요. 호랑이는 남매가 있는 곳에 점점 가까워졌어요. 남매는 너무 무서웠어요.
"오빠, 곧 잡힐 것 같아!"
오빠는 눈을 꼭 감고 기도하기 시작했어요.
"제발 저희를 살려 주세요."
남매가 호랑이에게 잡히기 바로 전이었어요. 기적처럼 하늘에서 동아줄이 쑥 내려왔어요. 남매는 얼른 동아줄에 매달렸어요. 동아줄은 남매를 데리고 하늘로 올라갔어요.

남매의 모습을 본 호랑이도 하늘에 기도했어요.
"저에게도 동아줄을 내려 주세요."

우물 well 비치다 to be reflected 나뭇잎 leaf 사라지다 to disappear 따르다 to follow
가까워지다 to get closer 꼭 tightly 기도하다 to pray 기적 miracle 동아줄 rope 쑥 mimetic word
describing something going up/down suddenly 매달리다 to grab onto 데리다 to take/bring someone

일상 속에서 진짜 자주 등장하는 한국 옛날이야기

"Hey kids, where are you?"

The siblings were reflected in the well in the backyard. The tiger thought that the siblings were inside the well and tried to go into the well.

Just then, a leaf fell from the tree and went into the well. The image of the siblings reflected in the well disappeared. The tiger realized that the siblings were not inside the well.

"Roar! They were not hiding in the well!"

The tiger found the siblings who were in the tree. And it started to climb up after them. The tiger got closer and closer to where the siblings were. The siblings were very scared.

"Brother, I think we are going to get caught soon!"

The brother closed his eyes and began to pray.

"Please save us."

The siblings were about to be caught by the tiger. As if by a miracle, a rope descended from the sky. The siblings quickly grabbed onto the rope. The rope lifted the siblings up to the sky.

The tiger also prayed to the sky after seeing the siblings.

"Please send down a rope for me, too."

하늘에서 또 동아줄이 내려왔어요. 호랑이도 얼른 동아줄에 매달렸어요. 동아줄이 호랑이와 함께 올라가기 시작했어요. 호랑이는 남매를 잡을 수 있다는 생각에 신이 났어요.

그때였어요. 호랑이가 매달려 있던 동아줄이 뚝 끊어졌어요.
"으악!"
호랑이는 그대로 땅으로 떨어져서 죽었어요. 호랑이에게 내려온 동아줄은 사실 썩은 동아줄이었어요. 하늘에서 착한 남매에게는 튼튼한 동아줄을 내려 주고, 못된 호랑이에게는 썩은 동아줄을 내려 준 거예요.

튼튼한 동아줄에 매달린 남매는 무사히 하늘로 올라갔어요. 그 후로 동생은 해기 되고 오빠는 딜이 되어 세상을 밝게 비추었다고 해요.

뚝 mimetic word describing something hard being broken or snapped 끊어지다 to snap
으악 sound of screaming 썩다 to rot, to be rotten 못되다 to be mean 무사히 safely 비추다 to shine

일상 속에서 진짜 자주 등장하는 한국 옛날이야기

Another rope came down from the sky. The tiger also grabbed onto the rope quickly. The rope began to rise up with the tiger. He was excited at the thought of being able to catch the siblings.

But then, the rope the tiger was holding onto suddenly snapped.
"Ahhh!"
The tiger fell straight to the ground and died. The rope that came down to the tiger was actually a rotten one. The kindhearted siblings had been given a sturdy rope from the sky, while the mean tiger had been given a rotten rope.

The siblings, who were hanging onto the sturdy rope, safely ascended into the sky. After that, the younger sibling became the sun and the older sibling became the moon, and they have been shining brightly upon the world ever since.

Comprehension Quiz

Read the statements below and mark them as true or false.

1. 어머니는 호랑이에게 떡을 주지 않았다. ——————— True / False

2. 여동생은 호랑이가 온 줄 모르고 문을 열었다. ——— True / False

3. 남매는 우물 안에 숨었다. ———————————— True / False

4. 호랑이는 남매가 있는 나무 위에 올라갔다. ———— True / False

5. 호랑이가 잡은 동아줄은 썩은 동아줄이었다. ——— True / False

Modern Application

" casual 떡 하나 주면 안 잡아먹지! (= If you give me one rice cake, I won't eat you!)" You will often hear this in Korea. Although the word "eat" may sound a little frightening, it's actually a cute way to ask someone for something, while concealing embarrassment and being a little naughty at the same time. You can replace 떡 with any kind of food or thing and say " casual 과자 하나 주면 안 잡아먹지! (= If you give me a cookie, I won't eat you!)", or you can put a phrase of request in place of a verb and say " casual 나 대신 설거지해 주면 안 잡아먹지! (= If you do the dishes for me, I won't eat you!)"

In this story, the rope that the tiger held was rotten and led to its death. So when your decision turns out to be not helpful or even makes things worse, you can say like "그게 썩은 동아줄인 줄도 모르고 잡았어요. (= I caught it without realizing that it was a rotten rope.)" or " casual 내가 잡은 게 썩은 동아줄이었어. (= I picked the rotten rope.)"

Example Dialogue (1)

지나: 라면 냄새 좋다. 나 한 입만.

준우: 좀 전엔 안 먹는다며.

지나: 그땐 안 먹고 싶었지. 진짜 라면 한 입만 주면 안 잡아먹을게.

Jina: Ramyeon smells good. Give me a bite.

Junu: You said you didn't want to eat it earlier.

Jina: I didn't want to eat it then. If you give me just one bite of
ramyeon, I won't devour you.

Example Dialogue (2)

소연: 내일 팀 과제 발표하는 날이지? 잘되고 있어?

동준: 아니. 어떤 사람이 파워포인트 잘한다길래 내가 같이 하자고
했는데, 며칠 전부터 연락이 안 돼. 오늘 밤 새워야 할 것 같아.

소연: 쯧쯧. 썩은 동아줄을 잡았네. 내가 도울 거 있으면 말해.

Soyeon: Tomorrow is the day you present the team project, right?
Is everything going well?

Dongjun: No. I asked someone who said he was good at
PowerPoint to work on the project with me, but I haven't
heard from him since a few days ago. I think I'll have to
stay up all night tonight.

Soyeon: Tsk tsk. You caught a rotten rope. If you need any help, let
me know.

Answers

1. False 2. False 3. False 4. True 5. True

06

No Bottom,
No Gain

How come?
Find out on the next page

콩쥐 팥쥐

옛날 어느 마을에 콩쥐라는 착한 여자아이가 아버지와 함께 살고 있었어요. 콩쥐의 어머니는
콩쥐가 어렸을 때 돌아가셨어요. 그러던 어느 날, 아버지가 새로 결혼을 하게 되면서 콩쥐에게
새어머니가 생겼어요. 새어머니에게는 팥쥐라는 딸이 있었어요.
"어머니, 안녕하세요? 팥쥐야, 안녕? 앞으로 사이좋게 지내자."
착한 콩쥐는 새어머니와 동생 팥쥐를 반갑게 맞았어요. 하지만 새어머니와 팥쥐는 콩쥐를
반가워하지 않았어요.

그런데 얼마 후, 콩쥐 아버지가 병으로 돌아가셨어요. 아버지가 돌아가시자 새어머니는 팥쥐만
예뻐하고, 콩쥐에게 힘든 집안일을 매일 시켰어요. 하루는 새어머니가 콩쥐를 불러 항아리에
물을 채우게 했어요.
"얘, 콩쥐야! 이 항아리에 물을 가득 채워라. 저녁때까지 다 못 하면 오늘 저녁밥도 없을 줄
알아!"
"네, 어머니."
콩쥐는 항아리에 물을 채우기 시작했어요. 그런데 아무리 물을 부어도 항아리에 물이 차지
않았어요.

여자아이 girl, baby girl 돌아가시다 to pass away 새어머니 stepmother 사이좋다 to be on good terms
맞다 to welcome, to greet 집안일 household chores 항아리 traditional Korean earthenware jar
채우다 to fill 얘 hey, kid 저녁때 evening 저녁밥 dinner 붓다 to pour

일상 속에서 진짜 자주 등장하는 한국 옛날이야기

Kongjwi and Patjwi

Once upon a time in a village, a kindhearted girl named Kongjwi lived with her father.
Kongjwi's mother had passed away when she was little. And then one day, her father
remarried, and Kongjwi gained a stepmother. The stepmother had a daughter named
Patjwi.
"Hello, Mother! Hello, Patjwi! Let us get along well from now on."
Kindhearted Kongjwi warmly welcomed her stepmother and younger sister, Patjwi.
However, the stepmother and Patjwi did not welcome Kongjwi.

But after some time, Kongjwi's father became ill and passed away. After his death, the
stepmother only favored Patjwi and made Kongjwi do all the difficult household chores
every day. One day, the stepmother called Kongjwi and asked her to fill a jar with water.
"Hey, Kongjwi! Fill up this jar with water. If you cannot finish it by evening, there will
not be any dinner for you tonight!"
"Yes, Mother."
Kongjwi began to fill the jar with water. However, no matter how much water she
poured, the jar did not fill up.

콩쥐 팥쥐

'이상하다. 왜 이렇게 물이 안 차지?'

항아리를 살펴보던 콩쥐는 항아리 바닥에 큰 구멍이 있는 걸 발견했어요. 못된 새어머니가 구멍이 있는 항아리에 물을 채우게 한 거였어요.

"앗! 구멍이 있었구나! 구멍이 있는 항아리에 어떻게 물을 가득 채우지? 오늘도 저녁밥을 먹지 못하겠어. 흑흑."

속상해하고 있는 콩쥐 앞에 두꺼비가 나타났어요.

"콩쥐 아가씨, 걱정하지 말아요. 제가 항아리 안에 들어가서 구멍을 막고 있을게요. 물을 얼른 채우세요."

"두꺼비야, 정말 고마워!"

두꺼비 덕분에 콩쥐는 항아리에 물을 가득 채울 수 있었어요. 그리고 그런 콩쥐에게 새어머니는 저녁밥을 줄 수밖에 없었어요.

며칠 뒤, 마을에서 큰 잔치가 열렸어요. 새어머니와 팥쥐는 잔치에 갈 준비를 하고 있었어요.

"어머니, 이 치마 어때요? 잘 어울려요?"

"정말 예쁘구나! 역시 우리 딸이 최고야!"

콩쥐는 팥쥐가 너무 부러워서 새어머니에게 말했어요.

"어머니, 저도 잔치에 가고 싶어요."

새어머니는 잠깐 생각하고는 말했어요.

"잔치? 그래, 좋다."

살펴보다 to examine 구멍 hole 발견하다 to discover 못되다 to be mean 앗 oh 흑흑 sound of sobbing 속상하다 to be upset 두꺼비 toad 얼른 quickly 잔치 feast 어울리다 to suit

"It is strange. Why isn't the water filling up?"

Kongjwi examined the jar and discovered a big hole at the bottom. It turned out that the mean stepmother made her fill a jar with a hole in it.

"Oh! There was a hole! How can I fill up a jar with water when it has a hole? Again, I will not be able to have dinner tonight. Sob, sob."

Kongjwi was upset when a toad appeared before her.

"Do not worry, Kongjwi. I will go inside the jar and block the hole. Please quickly fill it with water."

"Toad, thank you so much!"

Thanks to the toad, Kongjwi was able to fill the jar with water to the brim. And because of that, the stepmother had no choice but to give Kongjwi dinner.

A few days later, a grand feast was held in the village. The stepmother and Patjwi were getting ready to attend the feast.

"Mother, how does this skirt look? Does it suit me well?"

"It looks really beautiful! As always, my daughter is the best!"

Kongjwi felt envious of Patjwi and spoke to her stepmother.

"Mother, I want to go to the feast, too."

After a brief moment of thought, the stepmother replied, "The feast? Sure, why not."

"정말요?"

콩쥐는 너무 기뻤어요. 하지만 새어머니는 사실 콩쥐를 잔치에 데려갈 생각이 없었어요.

"대신 여기 있는 벼 껍질을 다 벗기고, 저기 있는 베도 다 짠 뒤에 잔치에 와라."

"네? 그걸 다요?"

"아니면 그냥 집에서 일하고 있을래? 다 잔치에 가면 누가 집안일을 해?"

"아니에요, 어머니. 다 해 놓고 잔치에 갈게요."

새어머니와 팥쥐는 콩쥐만 남겨 놓고 먼저 잔치에 갔어요.

콩쥐는 먼저 벼의 껍질을 벗기기 시작했어요.

"휴, 이 많은 걸 언제 다 하지?"

그때, 참새들이 나타나서 말했어요.

"콩쥐 아가씨, 걱정하지 말아요. 우리가 도와드릴게요."

"참새들아, 정말 고마워!"

참새들 덕분에 콩쥐는 벼의 껍질을 다 벗길 수 있었어요.

다음으로 콩쥐는 베를 짜기 시작했어요. 그런데 베를 짜는 건 정말 오래 걸리는 일이었어요. 콩쥐는 잔치에 못 가게 될 것 같아서 걱정되었어요. 그때, 하늘에서 선녀가 내려와 콩쥐에게 말했어요.

"콩쥐야, 내가 베를 짤 테니까 너는 어서 잔치에 갈 준비를 하렴. 여기 예쁜 옷과 신발이 있어."

"선녀님, 정말 감사해요!"

벼 rice 껍질 husk 벗기다 to peel off 베 hemp cloth 짜다 to weave 휴 phew 참새 sparrow

선녀 fairy in Korean fairy tales, usually wearing a dress

"Really?"

Kongjwi was overjoyed. However, in reality, the stepmother had no intention of taking Kongjwi to the feast.

"However, peel off all the husks from the rice here, and weave all the hemp cloth over there. Then come to the feast."

"What? All of that?"

"Or would you rather stay home and do the chores? If everyone goes to the feast, who will take care of the household work?"

"No, Mother. I will finish everything and go to the feast."

The stepmother and Patjwi left for the feast, leaving Kongjwi behind.

Kongjwi began peeling off the husks from the rice first.

"Phew, when am I going to finish all of this?"

At that moment, sparrows appeared and spoke.

"Do not worry, Kongjwi. We will help you."

"Sparrows, thank you so much!"

Thanks to the sparrows, Kongjwi was able to peel off all the rice husks.

Next, Kongjwi started weaving the hemp cloth. However, weaving the hemp cloth was a task that took a really long time. Kongjwi was worried that she would not be able to make it to the feast. Then, a fairy descended from the sky and spoke to Kongjwi.

"Kongjwi, I will weave the hemp cloth for you. You should prepare to go to the feast. Here are beautiful clothes and shoes for you."

"Fairy, thank you so much!"

선녀 덕분에 준비를 끝낸 콩쥐가 잔치에 달려가고 있었어요. 그때였어요.

"원님 지나가신다! 모두 비켜라!"

큰 소리에 놀란 콩쥐가 넘어지면서 신고 있던 신발이 강물에 빠졌어요.

"앗, 안 돼!"

그 소리를 듣고 콩쥐를 본 원님은 콩쥐에게 첫눈에 반했어요. 원님은 콩쥐를 부르려고 했어요. 하지만 당황한 콩쥐는 이미 사라진 후였어요. 원님은 강물에 떠 있는 콩쥐의 신발을 가리키며 신하들에게 말했어요.

"저 신발의 주인을 꼭 찾아 와라."

다음 날부터 원님의 신하들은 신발의 주인을 찾기 위해 온 마을을 돌아다녔어요. 하지만 그 신발의 주인을 찾을 수 없었어요.

"온 마을을 다 돌아다녔는데, 이 신발이 맞는 사람이 없네요. 저 집까지만 가 봅시다."

그 집은 콩쥐의 집이었어요. 원님이 이 신발의 주인을 찾는다고 하자, 새어머니는 콩쥐를 부엌으로 보내고 팥쥐에게 신발을 신어 보라고 했어요. 하지만 팥쥐의 발에는 신발이 맞지 않았어요. 그러자 신하들이 말했어요.

"아까 부엌으로 간 아가씨도 불러 주시겠어요?"

"그 아이는 이 신발의 주인이 아닐 거예요. 그 아이에게는 이런 예쁜 신발이 없어요."

원님 honorific *wonnim*, term used to address a local governor in the Joseon Dynasty   비키다 to make way   강물 river water   첫눈에 반하다 to fall in love at first sight   당황하다 to be flustered 사라지다 to vanish   신하 servant, retainer, subject   돌아다니다 to go around

Thanks to the fairy, Kongjwi finished her preparations and was rushing to the feast. And it was at that moment...

"*Wonnim* is passing by! Make way!"

Surprised by the loud voice, Kongjwi stumbled and the shoe she had been wearing fell into the river.

"Oh no!"

Upon hearing the sound and seeing Kongjwi, wonnim fell in love with her at first sight. Wonnim was about to call Kongjwi. However, flustered Kongjwi had already vanished. Pointing at Kongjwi's shoe floating in the river, wonnim instructed his servants.

"Find the owner of that shoe no matter what and bring her to me."

From the next day on, wonnim's servants searched the entire village to find the owner of the shoe. However, they could not find the owner of the shoe.

"We have searched the whole village, but there seems to be no one who fits the shoe. Let us just try one more house over there."

That house was Kongjwi's home. When they heard that wonnim was looking for the owner of the shoe, the stepmother sent Kongjwi to the kitchen and asked Patjwi to try on the shoe. However, the shoe did not fit Patjwi's foot. Then the servants suggested:

"Would you please also call the girl who went to the kitchen earlier?"

"That girl could not be the owner of this shoe. She does not have such pretty shoes."

원님의 신하들은 새어머니의 말을 듣지 않고, 콩쥐를 불러 신발을 신어 보게 했어요.

"어허! 원님이 시키신 일입니다. 아가씨, 여기로 와서 어서 이 신발을 신어 보세요!"

부엌에서 나온 콩쥐는 천천히 신발에 발을 넣었어요. 신발이 콩쥐의 발에 꼭 맞았어요.

"드디어 이 신발의 주인을 찾았군요! 아가씨, 원님이 이 신발의 주인을 찾고 계십니다. 저희와 함께 가시겠습니까?"

콩쥐는 웃으며 대답했어요.

"좋아요."

신하들은 콩쥐를 원님에게 데려갔어요. 원님은 콩쥐를 다시 만나게 되어 정말 기뻤어요.

"전에 내가 지나가는 소리에 놀라서 신발을 잃어버렸죠? 미안해요. 저는 그때 아가씨를 보고 첫눈에 반했어요."

콩쥐도 신발을 찾아 준 원님이 마음에 들었어요.

그렇게 콩쥐와 원님은 사랑에 빠졌고, 이후 두 사람은 많은 사람들의 축하 속에서 결혼해서 행복하게 살았다고 해요.

어허 sound that people make when they are displeased with someone who is younger or in a lower societal position   마음에 들다 to like   사랑에 빠지다 to fall in love

Wonnim's servants did not listen to the stepmother's words and called Kongjwi to try on the shoe.

"Hey! It is the task wonnim gave us. Miss, come here and try on this shoe immediately!"

Kongjwi, who came out of the kitchen, slowly put her foot into the shoe. The shoe fit perfectly on Kongjwi's foot.

"We have finally found the owner of this shoe! Miss, wonnim is looking for the owner of this shoe. Will you come with us?"

Kongjwi smiled and replied, "Of course."

The servants took Kongjwi to wonnim. Wonnim was overjoyed to see Kongjwi again.

"The other day, you lost your shoe because you were surprised by the sound of me passing by, right? I am sorry. I saw you then and fell in love at first sight."

Kongjwi also liked wonnim, who had found her shoe for her.

Just like that, Kongjwi and wonnim fell in love, and afterward, the two of them got married receiving much congratulation from many people, and they lived happily ever after.

Comprehension Quiz

Read the statements below and mark them as true or false.

1. 팥쥐는 콩쥐를 반가워했다. ———————————— True / False
2. 새어머니는 콩쥐를 잔치에 데려가고 싶어 했다. ———— True / False
3. 콩쥐가 물을 채워야 하는 항아리에는 큰 구멍이 있었다. —— True / False
4. 콩쥐가 벼의 껍질을 벗기는 것을 두꺼비들이 도와줬다. —— True / False
5. 원님은 콩쥐에게 첫눈에 반했다. ———————————— True / False

Modern Application

콩쥐 (Kongjwi) and 팥쥐 엄마 (the mother of Patjwi) are two of the most frequently mentioned characters from Korean folktales, even to this day. Kongjwi is a good-natured person who is always willing to help others or do favors for other people. Therefore, when someone works very hard without showing any hesitation or complaint or someone is forced to do a lot of hard work, you can describe him/her as Kongjwi.

On the other hand, the mother of Patjwi is a stepmother who is mean to Kongjwi. So mothers, not necessarily actual stepmothers, who are a bit strict with their children are often jokingly referred to as 팥쥐 엄마.

The proverb "밑 빠진 독에 물 붓기 (= Pouring water into a jar without a bottom)", which originated from this story, is also frequently quoted. 밑 빠진 독 means "a jar with a hole on the bottom", thus 밑 빠진 독에 물 붓기 is used to describe something that doesn't bear fruitful results in spite of the effort or time that went in, just as the jar without a bottom would never fill up.

민수: 새로 시작한 아르바이트는 어때?

다혜: 너무 힘들어. 내가 일 잘한다고 사장님이 일을 계속 주셔.

민수: 아이고, 이 콩쥐야. 열심히 하는 것도 좋지만 힘들면 힘들다고 말해야지.

Minsu: How's the new part-time job going?

Dahye: It's so tough. The boss keeps giving me more work because I'm good at it.

Minsu: Jeez, you poor Kongjwi. It's good to work hard, but if it's tough, you should speak up and say so.

Example Dialogue (2)

지나: 우리 엄마는 팥쥐 엄마인가 봐. 어제 나한테 설거지랑 방 청소까지 시키는 거 있지.

재석: 다 컸는데 그 정도는 해야지. 나중에 독립하면 다 도움이 될 거야.

지나: 나 지금 소름 돋았어. 우리 엄마랑 똑같이 말하네.

Jina: I think my mom is Patjwi's mom. Yesterday, she even had me do the dishes and clean the room.

Jaeseok: Well, now that you've grown up, you should do those things. It'll be helpful later when you live on your own.

Jina: I just got goosebumps. You sound exactly like my mom.

Example Dialogue (3)

세호: 너 왜 6과 공부하고 있어? 오늘 시험 5과 아니야?

수아: 선생님이 5과는 시험 안 본다고 하셨는데 못 들었어?

세호: 뭐? 어젯밤에 나 5과 진짜 열심히 공부했는데... 다 밑 빠진 독에 물 붓기였다니!

Seho: Why are you studying Lesson 6? Today's test is on Lesson 5, isn't it?

Sua: The teacher said we wouldn't have a test on Lesson 5. Didn't you hear?

Seho: What? I studied Lesson 5 really hard last night... Turns out I was pouring water into a jar without a bottom!

07

Uh-oh, This Is Unexpected

How come?
Find out on the next page

$\longrightarrow$

혹부리 할아버지

옛날에 턱 밑에 큰 혹이 달린 혹부리 할아버지가 살았어요. 할아버지는 마음씨가 착하고 노래를
잘 불렀어요.

어느 날, 착한 혹부리 할아버지는 나무를 구하려고 산에 갔어요. 할아버지는 열심히 나무를
주웠어요. 그런데 갑자기 하늘이 어두워지고, 빗방울이 떨어지기 시작했어요. 할아버지는 쉬어
갈 곳이 없는지 주위를 둘러보았어요.

그때, 저 멀리 집 하나가 보였어요. 가까이 가서 보니 아무도 살지 않는 허름한 집이었어요.
할아버지는 그 집에서 하룻밤 자고 가야겠다고 생각하고 집 안으로 들어갔어요. 그런데 아무도
없는 집에서 혼자 자려고 하니까 너무 무서웠어요. 그래서 할아버지는 노래를 부르기
시작했어요.
"달아, 달아, 밝은 달아. 달아, 달아, 밝은 달아!"
그때였어요.
"얼씨구절씨구, 좋구나! 좋다!"
누군가 할아버지를 칭찬했어요. 할아버지는 너무 놀라서 뒤를 돌아봤어요. 무섭게 생긴
도깨비들이 할아버지를 보고 있었어요.

혹부리 playful nickname for a person with a lump on one's face   턱 chin, jaw   혹 lump   달리다 to hang
마음씨 attitude, heart   구하다 to find, to look for   빗방울 raindrop   둘러보다 to look around
허름하다 to be shabby   하룻밤 one night   얼씨구절씨구 sympathetic response people make when
cheering to Korean traditional music   생기다 to look   도깨비 goblin

The Old Man with a Lump

Once upon a time, there lived an old man with a big lump under his chin. He was kindhearted and sang well.

One day, the kindhearted old man with a lump went to the mountain to find firewood. He worked hard to pick up wood, but suddenly the sky became dark, and raindrops began to fall. He looked around to see if there was any place to rest.

Then, he saw a house far away. When he checked it out up close, it turned out to be a shabby house where no one lived. The old man decided to spend the night there and went inside. However, he was scared to sleep alone in an empty house. So he started singing a song:
"Moon, moon, bright moon. Moon, moon, bright moon!"
Just then, "Woohoo! That is good! It sounds nice!"
Someone complimented the old man. The old man was really surprised and turned around. Some scary-looking goblins were looking at him.

혹부리 할아버지

"어떻게 그렇게 노래를 잘 부르는 거지? 어서 말해 봐!"

도깨비들이 무서운 표정으로 할아버지에게 물었어요. 할아버지는 너무 무서웠지만, 차분하게 생각했어요.

'대답을 잘못하면 죽을지도 몰라. 정신 차리자! 어떻게 말해야 여기서 무사히 나갈 수 있을까?'

그리고 곧 이렇게 말했어요.

"이 혹 보이세요? 사실, 이 혹이 바로 노래 주머니예요. 이 혹에서 노래가 나와요."

할아버지의 말에 한 도깨비가 말했어요.

"이 혹에서 노래가 나온다고? 그럼 그 혹을 우리에게 내놔. 대신 우리가 보물을 줄게."

도깨비는 할아버지의 대답은 듣지도 않고, 도깨비방망이로 할아버지의 혹을 툭 쳤어요.

그랬더니 할아버지의 혹이 떼어졌어요. 그리고 도깨비는 다시 방망이로 바닥을 툭 쳤어요.

그랬더니 온갖 보물이 나왔어요. 그렇게 착한 혹부리 할아버지는 좋아하지 않았던 혹도 떼고,

보물도 잔뜩 얻어서 집으로 돌아올 수 있었어요. 할아버지는 정말 행복했어요.

며칠 뒤, 착한 할아버지가 혹도 떼고 보물도 얻었다는 이야기를 이웃 마을 혹부리 할아버지가

들었어요. 이웃 마을의 혹부리 할아버지는 마음씨가 나쁘고 욕심이 많았어요. 욕심쟁이 혹부리

할아버지는 이미 부자였지만 더 부자가 되고 싶어서 착한 할아버지를 찾아갔어요. 착한

할아버지는 산에서 있었던 일을 모두 말해 줬어요.

표정 facial expression   차분하다 to be calm   정신을 차리다 to collect one's mind   무사히 safely

내놓다 to put   대신 in return, instead   보물 treasure   도깨비방망이 goblin's magic club   툭 sound of

hitting something lightly   떼다 to take something off   온갖 all kinds of   잔뜩 a lot   욕심 greed

욕심쟁이 disapproving/casual greedy person

"How can you sing so well? Go ahead and tell us!"

The goblins asked the old man with scary expressions. The old man was very scared, but he thought calmly.

"If I answer wrong, I might die. I need to think clearly. How can I answer so that I can leave here safely?"

And he soon spoke like this: "Do you see this lump? Actually, this lump is a singing pouch. Songs come out of this lump."

One of the goblins replied to the old man's words: "Songs come out of this lump? Then give us the lump. In return, we will give you treasure."

The goblin did not even listen to the old man's reply and tapped his lump with its magic club. Then the old man's lump came off. And then the goblin hit the ground with its magic club again, and all kinds of treasures came out. Just like that, the kindhearted old man with a lump was able to return home after removing the lump that he did not like and receiving a lot of treasure. The old man was very happy.

A few days later, another old man with a lump from a neighboring village heard the story of how the kindhearted old man had removed his lump and gained treasure.

The old man with a lump from the neighboring village was ill-natured and greedy. The greedy old man with a lump was already wealthy but wanted to become even richer, so he went to the kindhearted old man. The kindhearted old man told him everything that had happened on the mountain.

다음 날, 욕심쟁이 혹부리 할아버지는 당장 도깨비가 나온 집을 찾아갔어요. 깜깜한 밤이 되자 욕심쟁이 혹부리 할아버지는 노래를 불렀어요.

"달아, 달아, 밝은 달아. 달아, 달아, 밝은 달아!"

잠시 후, 밖에서 도깨비들이 오는 소리가 들렸어요. 욕심쟁이 혹부리 할아버지는 부자가 될 생각에 신났어요.

'이제 혹도 떼고, 큰 부자도 될 수 있겠구나!'

욕심쟁이 혹부리 할아버지는 도깨비들이 방에 들어오자마자 신이 나서 말했어요.

"제 노랫소리가 아주 아름답죠? 이 혹에서 아름다운 노래가 나오는 거예요. 이 혹을 가져가세요."

그런데 방으로 들어온 도깨비들은 욕심쟁이 혹부리 한아버지에게 크게 화를 냈어요.

"뭐? 혹에서 노래가 나와? 이 거짓말쟁이! 지난번에 준 혹도 가짜였잖아. 우리가 또 속을 줄 알아?"

"아니에요! 지난번에 혹을 준 건 제가 아니었어요!"

당황한 욕심쟁이 혹부리 할아버지가 말했지만, 도깨비들은 할아버지의 말을 듣지 않았어요.

"너 이놈! 지난번에 우리한테 준 혹도 다시 가져가라!"

도깨비들은 화가 나서 욕심쟁이 혹부리 할아버지의 턱에 혹을 하나 더 붙여 주었어요.

욕심쟁이 혹부리 할아버지는 울면서 마을로 돌아왔어요. 욕심쟁이 혹부리 할아버지는 부자가 되려고 욕심을 부리다가 혹만 하나 더 가지게 된 거예요.

당장 right away, immediately   깜깜하다 to be very dark   신나다 to be excited   노랫소리 singing voice
거짓말쟁이 liar   가짜 fake   속다 to be fooled   당황하다 to be flustered   이놈 brat
욕심을 부리다 to be greedy

The next day, the greedy old man with a lump went straight to the house where the goblins appeared. As the night grew darker, the greedy old man with a lump sang a song.

"Moon, moon, bright moon. Moon, moon, bright moon!"

Shortly after, he heard the sound of goblins coming from outside. The greedy old man with a lump was excited at the thought of becoming rich.

"Now I can get rid of my lump and become a wealthy man!"

As soon as the goblins entered the room, the greedy old man with a lump was so happy and said, "My singing voice is very beautiful, isn't it? Beautiful songs come out of this lump. Please take this lump."

However, the goblins who entered the room were very angry with the greedy old man with a lump.

"What? Songs come from this lump? You liar! The lump you gave us last time was fake. Do you think we will be fooled again?"

"No! That was not me who gave you the lump last time!" said the flustered greedy old man with a lump, but the goblins did not listen to him.

"You brat! Take back the lump you gave us last time!"

The goblins were angry and attached another lump to the greedy old man's chin.

The greedy old man with lumps returned to the village crying. He had been greedy for wealth and now only gained one more lump.

Comprehension Quiz

Read the statements below and mark them as true or false.

1. 착한 혹부리 할아버지는 노래를 부르러 산에 갔다. ⋯⋯⋯⋯⋯⋯ True / False

2. 착한 혹부리 할아버지는 도깨비가 무서웠다. ⋯⋯⋯⋯⋯⋯ True / False

3. 도깨비들은 혹이 노래 주머니라고 생각했다. ⋯⋯⋯⋯⋯⋯ True / False

4. 도깨비들은 노래가 듣기 싫어서 혹을 뗐다. ⋯⋯⋯⋯⋯⋯ True / False

5. 욕심쟁이 혹부리 할아버지는 혹이 두 개가 되었다. ⋯⋯⋯⋯ True / False

Modern Application

This story teaches us to be wary of excessive greed. The greedy old man with a lump tried to trick the goblins into removing his lump for him and giving him money, but he ended up getting scolded by the goblins and even getting another lump.

There is a famous saying that originated from this story: " casual 혹 떼러 갔다 혹 붙여 온다. (= You go to remove the lump, but come back with another lump.)" Another variation is " casual 혹 떼려다 혹 붙인다. (= You add another lump while trying to get rid of one.)" Both are widely used when someone is being overly greedy or when someone tries to manipulate a situation for one's own benefit, only to end up with a worse outcome.

Example Dialogue 🎧 Track 14

주희: 도윤 씨, 저녁에 뭐 해요?
도윤: 어, 음, 저 새로 나온 영화 보려고요!

주희: 어머, <혹부리 할아버지>요? 저도 그거 보고 싶었는데, 같이 볼래요?

도윤: 아, 하하... 그럴까요?

(주희가 간 뒤)

도윤: 혹 떼려다 혹 붙였네. 밥 먹자고 할까 봐 영화 본다고 한 건데.

Juhee: Doyoon, what are you doing tonight?

Doyun: Uh, um, I'm planning on watching a newly released movie!

Juhee: Oh, "The Old Man with a Lump"? I wanted to watch that, too.
Would you like to watch it together?

Doyun: Ah, haha... Shall we?

(After Juhee leaves)

Doyun: I wanted to get rid of my lump, but now I got another one.
Actually, I said I was going to watch a movie because I was
worried that she might ask me out to dinner.

08

Making a Long Distance Relationship Work

How come?
Find out on the next page →

견우와 직녀

아주 먼 옛날, 하늘 나라 임금님에게 직녀라는 딸이 있었어요. 직녀는 마음씨가 착하고, 베를 잘 짜는 걸로 유명했어요. 직녀가 짠 옷감은 반짝반짝 빛이 났어요. 직녀는 매일 부지런하게 베를 짰어요.

"직녀 공주님이 짠 옷감 좀 보세요! 반짝반짝 빛이 나죠?"

"직녀 공주님은 어쩜 저렇게 착하고 부지런하실까요?"

하늘 나라 사람들은 모두 직녀를 칭찬했어요.

그러던 어느 날, 직녀가 잠시 궁궐 밖으로 나갔다가 소를 몰고 있는 한 청년을 만나게 됐어요. 청년의 이름은 견우였어요. 견우는 하늘 나라에서 부지런하기로 유명한 농부였어요.

견우와 직녀는 처음 본 순간부터 서로 사랑에 빠졌어요. 곧 두 사람은 결혼을 하기 위해 하늘 나라 임금님을 찾아갔어요.

"아버지, 견우 님과 결혼하고 싶습니다. 허락해 주세요."

하늘 나라 임금님은 기쁜 마음으로 둘의 결혼을 허락했어요.

임금님 king 마음씨 attitude, heart 베 hemp cloth 짜다 to weave 옷감 cloth 반짝반짝 mimetic word describing something shining 빛이 나다 to shine 어쩜 how 궁궐 palace 몰다 to herd 청년 young man 농부 farmer 순간 moment 사랑에 빠지다 to fall in love 허락하다 to allow

Gyeonu and Jiknyeo

A long long time ago, the king of the heavenly kingdom had a daughter named Jiknyeo. She was known for her kind heart and excellent weaving skills. The clothes she wove shone brilliantly. She diligently weaved every day.

"Have a look at the clothes that Princess Jiknyeo has woven! They shine so brightly, don't they?"

"How can Princess Jiknyeo be so kind and diligent like that?"

Everyone in the kingdom of heaven praised Jiknyeo.

And then one day, while Jiknyeo was outside the palace, she met a young man herding cattle. His name was Gyeonu. He was a farmer that was well-known throughout the heavenly kingdom for his diligence.

Jiknyeo and Gyeonu fell in love at first sight, and soon after, they went to the king of the heavenly kingdom in order to get married.

"Father, I want to marry Gyeonu. Please allow it."

The king of the heavenly kingdom was pleased and gave his permission for the two to marry.

견우와 직녀

"직녀 공주님, 결혼 축하드려요!"

"견우 님, 축하해요!"

두 사람은 많은 사람들의 축하 속에서 결혼했어요.

"견우 님, 오늘은 우리 꽃을 보러 갈까요?"

"좋아요."

견우와 직녀는 결혼한 뒤에 매일 놀러 다니기만 했어요. 두 사람이 일을 하지 않는다는
이야기를 들은 임금님은 두 사람을 불러 혼을 냈어요.

"한 번만 용서해 주세요. 앞으로 일도 열심히 하겠습니다."

견우와 직녀는 임금님 앞에서 약속했어요. 하지만 곧 두 사람은 약속을 지키지 않고 다시 놀러
다니기 시작했어요.

견우는 계속 소를 돌보지 않았고, 직녀는 베를 짜지 않았어요. 결국 임금님은 두 사람을 다시
불렀어요.

"도저히 안 되겠다. 지금 당장 직녀는 은하수 서쪽으로, 견우는 은하수 동쪽으로 가라!"

하늘 나라 임금님은 견우와 직녀에게 벌을 내렸어요.

"잘못했어요. 한 번만 더 기회를 주세요."

견우와 직녀는 눈물을 흘리며 말했어요. 그 모습에 임금님은 마음이 약해졌어요.

"일 년에 한 번은 볼 수 있게 해 주겠다. 7월 7일에는 은하수를 사이에 두고 만나도록 해라."

혼을 내다 to scold　용서하다 to forgive　돌보다 to take care of　결국 eventually　도저히 (cannot) possibly
당장 immediately　은하수 the Milky Way　벌을 내리다 to punish　눈물을 흘리다 to shed tears
사이에 두다 to put something in between

일상 속에서 진짜 자주 등장하는 한국 옛날이야기

"Congratulations on your marriage, Princess Jiknyeo!"

"Congratulations, Gyeonu!"

The two got married amidst the congratulations of many people.

"Would you like to go see the flowers today, Gyeonu?"

"Sounds good."

After getting married, Gyeonu and Jiknyeo did nothing but just play every day. When the king heard that they were not doing any work, he brought them in and scolded them.

"Please forgive us just this once. We will also work hard from now on."

Gyeonu and Jiknyeo made a promise before the king. However, they soon broke their promise and started playing again.

Gyeonu continued to neglect his cows, and Jiknyeo stopped weaving. Eventually, the king called them back again.

"This is not working out. Jiknyeo, go to the west side of the Milky Way immediately, and Gyeonu, go to the east side of the Milky Way!"

The king of the heavenly kingdom punished Gyeonu and Jiknyeo.

"We were in the wrong. Please give us one more chance."

Gyeonu and Jiknyeo said with tears in their eyes. The sight made the king feel weak.

"I will allow you to meet once a year. Meet each other on July 7th with the Milky Way in between."

그렇게 견우와 직녀는 헤어지게 됐어요.

"견우 님! 견우 님!"

"공주님! 다시 만날 때까지 잘 지내야 해요!"

견우와 직녀는 7월 7일만 기다리면서 지냈어요. 견우는 열심히 농사를 지었고, 직녀는 열심히 베를 짰어요.

그리고 마침내 7월 7일이 됐어요. 견우와 직녀는 은하수로 달려갔어요. 두 사람은 은하수 바로 앞에 서서 서로를 찾았어요.

"직녀 공주님! 거기 계세요?"

그런데 은하수가 너무 넓어서 견우와 직녀는 서로의 얼굴을 볼 수 없었어요. 은하수를 건널 수 없었던 두 사람은 눈물을 흘리며 서로의 이름만 불렀어요.

"견우 님!"

"직녀 공주님!"

견우와 직녀가 흘린 눈물이 비로 변해 땅으로 떨어졌어요.

그렇게 매년 7월 7일이 되면 견우와 직녀는 아침 일찍부터 은하수로 달려갔어요. 두 사람은 서로의 이름을 부르며 눈물을 펑펑 흘렸어요. 두 사람의 눈물 때문에 땅에는 비가 아주 많이 내렸어요. 비 때문에 홍수가 나서 동물들이 살 집을 잃기도 했어요.

이렇게 7월 7일만 되면 홍수가 나자 동물들은 걱정이 많아졌어요.

"7월 7일마다 홍수가 나면 어쩌지?"

"무슨 좋은 방법이 없을까?"

마침내 finally   달려가다 to run   펑펑 mimetic word describing a large amount of liquid pouring at once
홍수가 나다 to flood

That is how Gyeonu and Jiknyeo had to part ways.

"Gyeonu! Gyeonu!"

"Princess! Take care until we meet again!"

Gyeonu and Jiknyeo spent all their time waiting for the 7th of July. Gyeonu worked hard on the farm, while Jiknyeo weaved diligently.

Finally, July 7th rolled around. Gyeonu and Jiknyeo ran to the Milky Way. They stood right in front of the Milky Way, trying to find each other.

"Princess Jiknyeo, are you there?"

However, the Milky Way was too wide, so Gyeonu and Jiknyeo could not see each other's faces. Not being able to cross the Milky way, they cried and just called out each other's names.

"Gyeonu!"

"Princess Jiknyeo!"

Their tears turned into rain and fell to the ground.

Just like that, every year on July 7th, Gyeonu and Jiknyeo ran to the Milky Way early in the morning. They cried while calling each other's names. Due to their tears, it rained heavily on the ground. The rain caused floods, and some animals even lost their homes.

Floods occurred like this whenever July 7th came around, so the animals became very worried.

"What if a flood happens every July 7th?"

"Is there any good solution?"

그때, 하늘 위를 날아다니던 까마귀와 까치가 말했어요.

"견우 님과 직녀 공주님이 만날 수 있도록 우리가 다리를 만들면 어떨까?"

"다리를 만든다고? 어떻게?"

"우리가 몸을 이어서 다리를 만들면 두 사람이 다리 위에서 만날 수 있을 거야. 그럼 두 사람이 울지 않을 거고, 홍수가 날 일도 없을 거야."

"와! 좋은 생각이야!"

7월 7일이 다시 돌아왔어요. 까마귀와 까치는 아침 일찍 은하수로 날아갔어요.

"자, 어서 다리를 만들자!"

"좋아! 좋아!"

까마귀와 까치는 서로의 몸을 이어서 다리를 만들었어요.

"견우 님, 직녀 공주님, 빨리 우리를 밟고 가세요!"

견우와 직녀는 까마귀와 까치가 만든 다리 위를 조심스럽게 걸어갔어요. 그리고 마침내 두 사람은 서로를 만날 수 있었어요.

"견우 님! 너무 보고 싶었어요."

"직녀 공주님, 저도요."

두 사람은 서로를 안으며 기뻐했어요.

까마귀와 까치가 만들어 준 다리 덕분에 견우와 직녀는 더 이상 울지 않았고, 홍수도 나지 않았어요. 그리고 이때부터 매년 7월 7일에 밤하늘을 보면 아주 밝게 빛나는 두 별을 볼 수 있는데, 견우와 직녀가 서로를 만나 기뻐서 밝게 빛나는 거라고 해요.

날아다니다 to fly around 까마귀 crow 까치 magpie 잇다 to connect 밟다 to step on

조심스럽다 to be careful 밤하늘 night sky

At that moment, crows and magpies flying in the sky said, "What if we build a bridge so that Gyeonu and Jiknyeo can meet?"

"Build a bridge? How?"

"If we connect our bodies to make a bridge, the two can meet on top of the bridge. Then they will not cry, and there will not be any floods."

"Wow! That is a great idea!"

July 7th came again. The crows and magpies flew to the Milky Way early in the morning.

"Let us make the bridge now!"

"Great! Great!"

The crows and magpies connected their bodies to make a bridge.

"Gyeonu, Princess Jiknyeo, hurry and go forth by stepping on us!"

Gyeonu and Jiknyeo walked carefully on the bridge the crows and magpies had made.

Finally, the two were able to meet each other.

"Gyeonu! I missed you so much."

"Princess Jiknyeo, me too."

They hugged each other and rejoiced.

Thanks to the bridge that the crows and magpies made, Gyeonu and Jiknyeo no longer cried, and there were no more floods. From then on, every year on July 7th, you can see two stars shining brightly in the night sky, which are said to be Gyeonu and Jiknyeo shining brightly because they are happy to see each other.

Comprehension Quiz

Read the statements below and mark them as true or false.

1. 직녀는 베를 잘 짰다. ———————————— True / False

2. 견우와 직녀는 결혼한 뒤에 일을 더 열심히 했다. ———— True / False

3. 견우와 직녀는 벌을 받아 7월 7일에만 만날 수 있다. ——— True / False

4. 견우와 직녀가 흘린 눈물이 비가 되어 홍수가 났다. ——— True / False

5. 견우와 직녀는 까마귀와 까치를 타고 날아서 만났다. ——— True / False

Modern Application

Have you ever heard of "오작교 (Ojakgyo)"? It's the bridge that the crows and magpies built by connecting their bodies in this story. Since Ojakgyo is the bridge that brings 견우 (Gyeonu) and 직녀 (Jiknyeo) together, Koreans metaphorically use the word Ojakgyo to describe someone who arranges marriages or romantic relationships between others. You might find this word in romance rumors of celebrities when referring to the matchmaker, and you can also use the expression "오작교 역할을 해 주다. (= to play the role of Ojakgyo)" in sentences.

In modern Korean society, Gyeonu and Jiknyeo are also often used to refer to a couple who can't meet frequently because they live far away from each other.

Example Dialogue (1)

예지: 너 요즘 수상해. 휴대폰 하면서 자꾸 웃고 말이야. 뭐 좋은 일 있어?

승완: 티 났어? 사실 나... 여자 친구 생겼어.

예지: 어쩐지! 언제부터? 누구야? 어떻게 만났어?

승완: 희주 고등학교 친구고, 한 달 정도 됐어. 희주가 오작교 역할을 해 줬지.

예지: 좋겠다. 부럽다. 나도 희주한테 소개해 달라고 할 거야.

Yeji: You've been acting suspicious lately. You keep smiling while looking at your phone. Is something good happening?

Seung-wan: Can you tell? Actually... I got a girlfriend.

Yeji: That's why! Since when? Who is she? How did you meet her?

Seung-wan: She's Heeju's high school friend, and it's been about a month. Heeju was our matchmaker.

Yeji: That's great! I'm jealous. I'll ask Heeju to introduce me to someone, too.

Example Dialogue (2)

수아: 아, 남자 친구 보고 싶다.

민호: 보면 되지.

수아: 그러고 싶지. 근데 남자 친구가 제주도에 살아.

민호: 제주도? 견우와 직녀가 따로 없네.

Sua: Ah, I miss my boyfriend.

Minho: Then go see him.

Sua: I want to, but my boyfriend lives on Jeju Island.

Minho: Jeju Island? It's like the story of Gyeonu and Jiknyeo being separated.

09

Confidence Maketh a Con Man

How come?
Find out on the next page

대동강을 판 김 선달

옛날에 다른 사람들을 잘 속이는 것으로 유명한 한 선달이 살고 있었어요. 그 선달의 성이 김 씨여서 사람들은 그를 '김 선달'이라고 불렀어요.

하루는 김 선달이 살고 있는 동네에 한양에서 온 상인들이 왔어요. 상인들은 한양에서보다 두 배 비싼 가격에 물건을 팔았어요.
"동전 여섯 개? 이건 한양에서 동전 세 개면 살 수 있는 거잖아요!"
김 선달의 말을 듣고 상인이 말했어요.
"물건 가격은 파는 사람 마음 아니에요? 싫으면 한양에서 사세요."
김 선달은 어쩔 수 없이 동전 여섯 개를 줬지만, 한양 상인들이 너무 얄미웠어요. 물건을 비싸게 파는 한양 상인들을 골탕 먹이고 싶었어요.

그러던 어느 날이었어요. 김 선달이 대동강 앞을 지나가고 있었어요. 김 선달의 눈에 열심히 대동강 물을 푸고 있는 사람들이 보였어요. 김 선달의 눈빛이 반짝였어요.
"아! 저 방법이 있었구나!"

대동강 the Daedong River, the name of a large river in North Korea   선달 *seondal*, person who passed the civil service examination but does not have a government position yet under the Joseon Dynasty
속이다 to trick   한양 *Hanyang*, the name of Seoul during the Joseon Dynasty   상인 merchant
얄밉다 to be unlikable or annoying because one is too smart or cunning   골탕 먹이다 to put someone through trouble   푸다 to scoop   눈빛 eyes, look in one's eyes   반짝이다 to sparkle

Seondal Kim Who Sold the Daedong River

Once upon a time, there lived a *seondal* who was famous for being very good at tricking other people. His family name was Kim, so people called him "Seondal Kim".

One day, merchants from *Hanyang* came to the town where Kim lived. They sold their goods at twice the price they sold them for in Hanyang.
"Six coins? You can buy this for only three coins in Hanyang!"
The merchant replied after listening to what Kim said, "The price of goods depends on the seller's desire, doesn't it? If you do not like it, go buy it in Hanyang."
Kim had no choice but to give them six coins, but he found the merchants from Hanyang annoying. He wanted to take revenge on the Hanyang merchants, who were selling their goods at high prices.

Then one day, as Kim was passing in front of *the Daedong River*, he saw people working hard to scoop water from the river. Kim's eyes sparkled.
"Ah! I can use that method!"

그날 밤, 김 선달은 대동강 물을 푸던 사람들을 모두 집으로 불렀어요.

"제가 지금 동전을 나눠 줄 테니 내일부터 물을 풀 때마다 저에게 동전을 돌려주고 가세요."

김 선달의 말에 사람들이 어리둥절한 표정을 지었어요.

"네? 왜 그런 일을 합니까?"

한 사람이 물었어요.

"나중에 다 알게 될 거예요. 혹시 누가 돈을 왜 내는 거냐고 물으면, 대동강 주인이 저라고

말하세요."

"뭐, 어려운 것도 아니니까 그렇게 하겠습니다."

다음 날, 김 선달은 대동강 앞에 책상과 의자를 놓고 앉았어요. 사람들은 김 선달과 약속한 대로

물을 풀 때마다 김 선달에게 동전을 냈어요. 그때 마침, 한양에서 온 상인들이 대동강 앞을

지나갔어요. 상인들은 사람들이 김 선달에게 돈을 내고 물을 사는 모습을 봤어요.

"왜 물을 푼 다음 저 사람에게 돈을 내는 걸까요?"

"그러게요."

상인들은 어리둥절해하며 대동강 앞을 지나갔어요.

다음 날도 사람들은 물을 풀 때마다 김 선달에게 돈을 냈어요. 어제와 같은 모습에 궁금해진 한

상인이 돈을 내고 지나가는 사람에게 물었어요.

어리둥절하다 to be puzzled   표정을 짓다 to make a (certain) look   마침 just, just in time

일상 속에서 진짜 자주 등장하는 한국 옛날이야기

That night, Kim invited all the people who were scooping water from the Daedong River to his house.

"I will hand out coins now, so from tomorrow, every time you scoop water, give me the coins back before you leave."

The people looked puzzled at Kim's words.

"What? Why do we have to do that?" asked one person.

"You will find out everything later. If anyone asks why you are paying, tell them that I am the owner of the Daedong River."

"Well, it is not difficult, so we will do as you say."

The next day, Kim set up a desk and a chair in front of the Daedong River and sat there. As promised, people paid him coins every time they scooped water. Just then, the merchants from Hanyang passed in front of the Daedong River. The merchants saw people paying money and buying water from Kim.

"Why are they paying him after scooping water?"

"I do not know."

The merchants passed in front of the Daedong River, feeling puzzled.

The following day, people again paid Kim every time they scooped water. One merchant who had become intrigued by the same situation from the day before asked a person who was passing by after paying.

"왜 저 사람에게 돈을 내는 거예요?"

"그거야 저분이 이 강의 주인이니까요."

그 사람은 김 선달과 약속한 대로 대답했어요.

"아니, 강에 주인이 있다고요?"

상인들은 매우 놀랐어요.

"우리는 한양에서 이렇게 먼 곳까지 힘들게 와서 돈을 버는데, 대동강 주인이라는 사람은
편하게 돈을 버네요."

"심지어 대동강은 일 년 내내 마르지 않는다고 해요. 너무 부럽네요."

다른 상인들의 말을 듣고 있던 한 상인이 말했어요.

"우리가 대동강을 사면 어때요?"

"네? 대동강을 산다고요? 아주 비쌀 것 같은데요."

"우리가 가지고 있는 돈을 합치면 되지요. 대동강을 살 수만 있다면 지금보다 훨씬 돈을 많이 벌
수 있을 거예요."

"오! 좋은 생각이에요. 내일 바로 대동강 주인이라는 사람을 만나 봅시다!"

한양에서 온 상인들은 김 선달에게 대동강을 사기로 결심했어요.

다음 날, 상인들은 대동강 앞에 앉아 있는 김 선달에게 다가갔어요.

"안녕하세요, 혹시 이 강의 주인이신가요?"

"그런데요. 무슨 일이죠?"

"우리는 한양에서 온 상인들입니다. 저희가 이 강을 사고 싶습니다."

심지어 even 내내 throughout 마르다 to dry, to go dry 합치다 to combine 결심하다 to decide,
to make up one's mind 다가가다 to approach

"Why are you paying that person money?"

"Well, that is because he is the owner of this river."

The person replied just as he had promised Kim.

"What? The river has an owner?"

The merchants were very surprised.

"We came all the way from Hanyang to earn money, and this guy who owns the Daedong River earns money so easily."

"Moreover, they say that the Daedong River never dries up all year round. I am so envious."

One of the merchants, who was listening to other merchants' conversation, said,

"What if we buy the Daedong River?"

"What? Buy the Daedong River? It seems very expensive."

"If we combine the money we have, we can. If we can buy the Daedong River, we will be able to make much more money than now."

"Oh! That is a good idea. Let us meet the person who is said to be the owner of the Daedong River tomorrow!"

The merchants from Hanyang decided to buy the Daedong River from Kim.

The next day, the merchants approached Kim, who was sitting in front of the Daedong River.

"Hello, are you the owner of this river by any chance?"

"Well, yes. What is the matter?"

"We are merchants from Hanyang and we want to buy this river."

상인들의 말에 김 선달은 크게 화를 냈어요.

"이 강은 함부로 팔 수 있는 그런 강이 아니에요! 돌아가신 부모님께 받은 강이란 말이에요!"

김 선달이 화를 내자 상인들이 얼른 말했어요.

"잠시만요. 우리는 한양에서 큰돈을 가지고 왔어요. 원하는 대로 돈을 드릴 수 있습니다."

한양 상인들은 대동강을 살 수만 있다면 가지고 있는 돈을 모두 다 써도 상관없다고
생각했어요.

"원하는 대로란 말이죠? 흠... 대동강은 아주 크고, 깨끗하고, 일 년 내내 마르지 않는 강이에요."

"알죠, 알죠. 그래서 얼마면 됩니까?"

김 선달은 고민하는 척하며 말했어요.

"적어도 동전 십만 개는 받아야 돌아가신 부모님께 죄송하지 않을 것 같아요."

"동, 동전 십만 개요?"

상인들이 생각한 것보다 훨씬 비싼 가격이었어요. 상인들이 잠깐 고민하자 김 선달이 다시
말했어요.

"이 정도면 싼 편인데, 싫으면 말고요. 대동강을 사고 싶어 하는 사람은 많아요. 어제도 한
사람이..."

"좋아요! 우리가 사겠습니다. 여기 동전 십만 개입니다."

김 선달이 다른 사람에게 대동강을 팔까 봐 마음이 급해진 상인들은 바로 동전 십만 개를 주고
대동강을 샀어요.

함부로 indiscreetly 돌아가시다 to pass away 얼른 quickly 큰돈 a lot of money 상관없다 to not care,

to not matter 적어도 at least 십만 a hundred thousand

Kim got very angry at the merchants' words.

"This is not a river that can be sold so easily! It is a river that my deceased parents gave me!"

When Kim got angry, the merchants quickly spoke up.

"Wait a minute. We brought a lot of money from Hanyang. We can give you as much as you want."

The Hanyang merchants thought they could spend all the money they had if they could just buy the Daedong River.

"As much as I want? Hmmm... The Daedong River is very big, clean, and does not dry up all year round."

"Yes, yes, we know that. So, how much do you want?"

Kim pretended to put a lot of thought into it and said, "I think I need at least 100,000 coins to not feel sorry to my deceased parents."

"100,000 coins?"

It was a much more expensive price than the merchants had thought. When the merchants hesitated for a moment, Kim spoke again.

"This is actually a pretty cheap price. If you do not like it, you can leave it. There are many people who want to buy the Daedong River. Yesterday, one person..."

"Okay! We will buy it. Here are 100,000 coins."

The merchants, who were anxious about the possibility of Kim selling the Daedong River to someone else, immediately gave him 100,000 coins and bought the river.

그리고 바로 다음 날, 상인들은 김 선달이 했던 것처럼 대동강 앞에 책상과 의자를 놓고
앉았어요. 마침 사람들이 물을 푸려고 대동강에 나타났어요. 상인들은 사람들이 돈을 내기만
기다렸어요. 그런데 사람들은 돈을 내지 않고 상인들 앞을 지나갔어요.

"저기요! 물을 펐으면 돈을 내야죠. 이제부터 이 강의 주인은 김 선달이 아니라 우리입니다."

상인의 말에 사람들은 어이없다는 표정을 지으면서 말했어요.

"강에 주인이 어디 있습니까? 우리는 김 선달 님에게 받은 돈을 다시 드린 것뿐이에요."

상인들은 그제야 김 선달에게 속았다는 것을 알게 됐어요. 하지만 이미 김 선달은 도망가고
없었어요. 그 후 김 선달은 주인이 없는 대동강을 팔아 큰돈을 번 사기꾼으로 아주
유명해졌다고 해요.

어이없다 to be dumbfounded   그제야 only after, only then   도망가다 to run away   사기꾼 swindler

And on the very next day, just like Kim had done, the merchants set up a desk and chairs in front of the Daedong River and sat there. Just then, people showed up at the river to scoop water. The merchants waited for them to pay for the water, but they just walked past them without paying.

"Excuse me! You should pay if you are scooping water. From now on, the owner of this river is not Kim, but us."

People looked dumbfounded and said, "How can there be an owner of a river? We were just returning the money we had received from Kim."

The merchants realized that they had been tricked by Kim. However, Kim had already run away and was nowhere to be found. After that, Kim became very famous as a swindler who made a lot of money by selling the ownerless Daedong River.

Comprehension Quiz

Read the statements below and mark them as true or false.

1. 한양 상인들은 물건을 싸게 팔았다. — True / False
2. 김 선달은 물을 푸는 사람들에게 동전을 미리 나눠 줬다. — True / False
3. 김 선달은 대동강의 진짜 주인이다. — True / False
4. 한양 상인들은 동전 십만 개를 주고 대동강을 샀다. — True / False
5. 물을 푸는 사람들이 한양 상인들에게도 돈을 냈다. — True / False

Modern Application

In Korea, 김 선달 (Seondal Kim) is more often referred to as 봉이 김 선달, with his nickname 봉이 (Bong-i) added. Seondal Kim was a man who lied and scammed people, so when someone shamelessly lies or sells something overpriced, you can say " [casual] 봉이 김 선달 같다. (= He/She's like Bong-i Seondal Kim.)" or " [casual] 김 선달도 아니고... (= You're not Seondal Kim. (So don't do this.))" Also, when the price of a product is so high that it's almost like a scam, you can say " [casual] 대동강 물 팔아먹는 수준이네. (= It's like selling water from the Daedong River.)" or " [casual] 대동강 물 팔아먹은 김 선달보다 더 하네. (= He/She's worse than Seondal Kim who sold water from the Daedong River.)"

Example Dialogue (1) Track 18

현우: 원래 10만 원이던 신발을 80만 원에 팔아? 이거 사기 아니야?

경화: 요새 유행하는 신발이어서 그래. 비싸긴 해도 진짜 예쁘지 않아?

현우: 아무리 그래도 이 가격은 진짜 아니야. 대동강 물 팔아먹는 수준이잖아.

Hyunwoo: These shoes were originally 100,000 won, and they're selling them for 800,000 won? Isn't this a scam?

Kyung-hwa: It's because those shoes are popular these days. They're expensive, but aren't they really pretty?

Hyunwoo: Even so, this price is just not reasonable. It's like selling water from the Daedong River.

Example Dialogue (2)

다혜: 이거 얼마예요?

수호: 5만 원만 주세요.

다혜: 네? 이거 하나에 무슨 5만 원이에요?

수호: 저희도 남는 거 없어요.

다혜: 아까 저 사람들한테는 3만 원에 파는 거 봤어요. 김 선달도 아니고 왜 사기를 치세요?

Dahye: How much is this?

Suho: Just give me 50,000 won.

Dahye: What? Is it 50,000 won for only this one item?

Suho: We're also barely making any profit on it.

Dahye: I saw you selling the same thing to those people earlier for 30,000 won. You're not Seondal Kim. Why are you trying to rip me off?

10

Don't Be Greedy, Bro!

How come?
Find out on the next page

흥부와 놀부

옛날 어느 마을에 흥부와 놀부 형제가 살고 있었어요. 동생 흥부는 착했지만, 형 놀부는 욕심이 많았어요.

그러던 어느 날, 흥부와 놀부의 아버지가 돌아가셨어요. 아버지는 돌아가시기 전에 이렇게 말씀하셨어요.
"놀부야, 흥부야, 사이좋게 지내야 한다. 재산은 꼭 둘이 나누어 가져라."
하지만 욕심쟁이 놀부는 아버지의 말을 듣지 않고 재산을 모두 차지했어요. 그리고 흥부네 가족들을 집에서 모두 내쫓았어요.

흥부네 가족들은 산 밑에 오두막집을 짓고 살게 되었어요. 흥부는 가족들을 위해 먹을 것을 구하려고 했지만, 겨울이라 먹을 것을 구하기가 어려웠어요.
"아버지, 배고파요."
"아버지, 집에 먹을 게 아무것도 없어요."
아무것도 먹지 못하고 있는 아이들을 보자 흥부는 마음이 아팠어요.
"안 되겠어요, 여보. 오늘은 형님 집에 찾아가 볼게요."
흥부는 어쩔 수 없이 놀부를 찾아갔어요.

욕심 greed 돌아가시다 to pass away 사이좋다 to be on good terms 재산 property, wealth
욕심쟁이 disapproving/casual greedy person 차지하다 to possess, to take 내쫓다 to kick out
오두막집 shack 짓다 to build 구하다 to find 배고프다 to be hungry 여보 honey (to one's wife or husband) 형님 honorific older brother

Heungbu and Nolbu

Once upon a time in a village, there lived two brothers named Heungbu and Nolbu.
Heungbu, the younger brother, was kindhearted, but Nolbu, the older brother, was very
greedy.

And then one day, their father passed away. Before he passed away, he said,
"Nolbu and Heungbu, live in harmony and divide the inheritance equally."
However, greedy Nolbu did not listen and took all the inheritance for himself. He then
kicked Heungbu and his family out of their house.

Heungbu and his family built a shack at the foot of a mountain and lived there. Heungbu
tried to find food for his family, but it was difficult because it was winter.
"Father, I am hungry."
"Father, there is nothing to eat at home."
Seeing his children not being able to eat anything, Heungbu felt heartbroken.
"I cannot take it anymore, honey. Today, I will visit my brother's house."
Heungbu had no other choice but to go to Nolbu's house.

"형님, 아이들이 굶고 있습니다. 제발 쌀을 조금만 주세요."

"너 이놈! 여기가 어디라고 와!"

욕심 많은 놀부는 빗자루를 들고 달려가서 흥부를 때렸어요. 욕심 많은 놀부의 부인도 주걱으로
흥부의 뺨을 찰싹 때렸어요. 그러자 주걱에 붙어 있던 밥알이 흥부의 뺨에 달라붙었어요.
흥부는 너무 배가 고파서 뺨에 붙은 밥알을 먹었어요. 흥부는 아이들을 위해 밥알을 더
얻으려고 다른 쪽 뺨도 내밀었어요.

"형수님, 이쪽 뺨도 주걱으로 때려 주세요."

"뭐? 당장 나가지 못해?"

흥부는 결국 밥알도 얻지 못하고 집으로 돌아가야 했어요.

시간이 흘러 봄이 되었어요. 제비 한 쌍이 흥부네 지붕 밑에 둥지를 짓고 알을 낳았어요. 곧
새끼 제비들이 태어났어요.

어느 날, 새끼 제비 한 마리가 둥지에서 떨어져 다리를 다쳤어요. 흥부는 새끼 제비의 다리를 잘
치료해 주었어요. 착한 흥부 덕분에 새끼 제비는 건강하게 자랐어요.

가을이 되자, 제비 가족은 흥부네 집을 떠나 따뜻한 곳으로 갈 준비를 했어요.

"조심히 가! 내년에 꼭 다시 와야 해!"

흥부는 떠나는 제비 가족을 바라보며 말했어요.

굶다 to starve   이놈 brat   빗자루 broom   달려가다 to run   때리다 to hit   주걱 (rice) paddle
뺨 cheek   찰싹 sound of a slap   밥알 grain of cooked rice   달라붙다 to stick   내밀다 to stick out
형수 one's elder brother's wife   당장 right now   결국 in the end   시간이 흐르다 time passes
제비 swallow   쌍 pair   지붕 roof   둥지 nest   알 egg

"Brother, my children are starving. Please give us some rice."

"You brat! How dare you come here!"

Greedy Nolbu ran over to Heungbu with a broom and hit him. Nolbu's greedy wife also slapped Heungbu's cheek with a rice paddle. Then, grains of rice from the paddle stuck to Heungbu's cheek. Heungbu was so hungry that he ate the rice stuck on his cheek. Heungbu then stuck out his other cheek to get more rice for the children.

"Sister-in-law, please hit my other cheek with the paddle."

"What? Get out right now!"

In the end, Heungbu could not get any more rice and had to go back home.

Time passed, and spring came. A pair of swallows built a nest under Heungbu's roof and laid eggs. Soon, baby swallows were born.

One day, one of the baby swallows fell from the nest and injured its leg. Heungbu took good care of the baby swallow's leg, and the baby swallow grew up healthily thanks to kindhearted Heungbu.

When autumn came, the swallow family prepared to leave from Heungbu's house for a warm place.

"Be careful and be sure to come back next year!"

Heungbu said as he watched the departing swallow family.

흥부와 놀부

다음 해 봄, 제비 가족이 흥부네 집에 다시 왔어요. 그런데 제비 한 마리가 흥부의 머리 위를 빙글빙글 돌다가 입에 물고 있던 무언가를 툭 떨어뜨렸어요. 박씨였어요. 그 모습을 본 흥부의 아들이 말했어요.

"아버지, 작년에 아버지가 치료해 준 제비예요! 제비가 박씨를 가져왔어요. 우리한테 주는 선물인가 봐요!"

흥부는 제비가 선물한 박씨를 땅에 심고 열심히 길렀어요.

가을이 되자 커다란 박들이 주렁주렁 열렸어요. 흥부 부부는 박을 하나 따서 자르기 시작했어요. 반 정도 잘랐을 때, 펑 소리와 함께 박이 갈라지더니 그 안에서 쌀이 쏟아져 나왔어요. 흥부는 깜짝 놀랐어요.

"아니, 이게 웬 쌀이야?"

흥부 부부는 너무 기뻤어요. 얼른 다른 박도 잘라 보았어요. 이번에는 펑 소리와 함께 박 속에서 보물이 쏟아져 나왔어요.

"세상에! 여보, 빨리 다른 박도 열어 봐요!"

그다음 박에서는 커다란 집이 나왔어요. 또 그다음 박에서는 수많은 하인이 나와 흥부에게 인사했어요. 그렇게 흥부는 하루 만에 마을에서 가장 큰 부자가 됐어요.

빙글빙글 round and round, in circles 물다 to have something in one's mouth 툭 sound of something dropping 떨어뜨리다 to drop 박씨 gourd seed 커다랗다 to be big 박 gourd 주렁주렁 mimetic word describing fruits hanging in clusters 열리다 (fruit) to appear/grow (on the tree) 따다 to pick 펑 bang 갈라지다 to split 쏟아져 나오다 to pour out 웬 what, why 얼른 quickly 보물 treasure 세상에 oh my 그다음 the next 수많다 to be numerous 하인 servant

일상 속에서 진짜 자주 등장하는 한국 옛날이야기

The next spring, the swallow family returned to Heungbu's house. However, one of
the swallows flew in circles above Heungbu's head and dropped something that it was
holding in its mouth. It was a gourd seed. Heungbu's son saw this and said, "Father, it
is the swallow you healed last year! The swallow brought a gourd seed. I guess it is a
gift for us!"
Heungbu planted the gourd seed that the swallow gifted him and grew it carefully.

In the autumn, large gourds grew and hung in clusters. Heungbu and his wife picked
a gourd and started to cut it. When they cut it about halfway, it split open with a loud
bang, and rice poured out from inside. Heungbu was surprised.
"Where did this rice come from?"
Heungbu and his wife were very happy. They quickly tried cutting open another gourd.
This time, with a loud bang, treasure poured out from inside the gourd.
"Oh, my! Honey, let us open the other gourds quickly!"
From the next gourd came out a large house. And from the next gourd, many servants
came out and greeted Heungbu. In this way, Heungbu became the richest person in
the village in just one day.

흥부의 소식을 들은 놀부가 흥부를 찾아왔어요. 놀부는 흥부가 부자가 된 것이 너무 부럽고 질투가 났어요. 놀부는 흥부에게 어떻게 부자가 되었는지 물었어요. 착한 흥부는 놀부에게 지금까지 있었던 일들을 모두 말해 주었어요.

흥부의 이야기를 들은 놀부는 산으로 올라가 제비를 찾아다녔어요. 마침 제비 한 마리를 발견했어요. 욕심 많은 놀부는 제비의 다리를 일부러 부러뜨렸어요. 그리고 제비의 다리를 치료해 주었어요.
"내가 다리를 치료해 주었으니 내년 봄에 꼭 박씨를 물어 와야 한다. 흐흐."

다음 해 봄, 제비가 정말로 놀부를 찾아와 박씨를 주었어요. 놀부는 신이 나서 박씨를 심고 열심히 길렀어요.

가을이 되자 놀부네 집에도 박이 주렁주렁 열렸어요.
"이제 내가 세상에서 제일 큰 부자가 될 거야."
놀부는 부인과 함께 박을 자르기 시작했어요. 반 정도 잘랐을 때, 펑 소리와 함께 박이 갈라졌어요. 그런데 박 속에서 나온 건 보물이 아니라 무서운 도깨비들이었어요. 도깨비들은 못된 놀부를 혼내 주고 놀부의 집도 부쉈어요. 놀부는 하루 만에 거지가 되었어요.

질투가 나다 to be jealous   찾아다니다 to go in search for   마침 just, just in time   발견하다 to find
일부러 purposely   부러뜨리다 to break   흐흐 sound of laughing wickedly or cunningly   정말로 really
신이 나다 to be excited   도깨비 goblin   못되다 to be mean   혼내다 to scold   부수다 to destroy
거지 beggar

Upon hearing the news of Heungbu, Nolbu came to see him. Nolbu was so envious and jealous that Heungbu became rich. He asked Heungbu how he became rich, and kindhearted Heungbu told him everything that had happened to him.

After hearing Heungbu's story, Nolbu went up to the mountain and searched for swallows. He happened to find one and purposely broke its leg out of greed. He then treated the swallow's leg.
"Since I have treated your leg, you must bring me a gourd seed next spring. Hehe."

The next spring, the swallow really came back to Nolbu and gave him a gourd seed. Excited, Nolbu planted the gourd seed and grew it diligently.

When autumn came, gourds grew in clusters in Nolbu's house as well.
"Now I will become the richest man in the world",
Nolbu began to cut a gourd with his wife. When they had cut it about halfway, the gourd split open with a loud bang. But instead of treasure, what came out of the gourd were scary goblins. The goblins punished Nolbu for being mean and destroyed his house. Nolbu became a beggar in just one day.

"흑흑. 내가 동생한테 못되게 해서 벌을 받았나 봐."

"그러게 말이에요. 우리 이제 어쩌죠?"

놀부와 놀부의 부인은 흥부에게 못되게 행동한 걸 반성했어요. 그때, 놀부의 소식을 들은 착한
흥부가 놀부의 집으로 달려왔어요. 흥부는 거지가 된 놀부에게 말했어요.

"형님, 걱정하지 마세요. 이제 저희 가족이랑 같이 살아요."

"동생아, 정말 미안하다. 내가 잘못했어."

놀부는 진심으로 흥부에게 사과했어요. 착한 흥부는 놀부를 용서하고 집으로 놀부 가족들을
데리고 왔어요. 그리고 흥부와 놀부는 함께 오순도순 사이좋게 살았어요.

흑흑 sound of sobbing 벌 punishment 반성하다 to reflect on 달려오다 to come running
진심 one's heart, one's true feelings 사과하다 to apologize 용서하다 to forgive 데리다 to take/bring
someone 오순도순 mimetic word describing people getting along well with each other

"Boo hoo. I guess I received punishment for treating my younger brother badly."

"That is right. What should we do now?"

Nolbu and his wife reflected on their bad behavior towards Heungbu. At that moment, kindhearted Heungbu, upon hearing the news about Nolbu, rushed to his house. Heungbu said to Nolbu, who had become a beggar, "Brother, do not worry. From now on, you can live together with my family."

"Younger brother, I am really sorry. I was in the wrong."

Nolbu sincerely apologized to Heungbu. Kindhearted Heungbu forgave Nolbu and brought Nolbu's family back to his house. From then on, Heungbu and Nolbu lived happily together.

흥부와 놀부

Comprehension Quiz

Read the statements below and mark them as true or false.

1. 놀부는 욕심이 많다. —————————————— True / False

2. 흥부는 놀부의 형이다. —————————————— True / False

3. 흥부는 새끼 제비의 다리를 치료해 주었다. ————— True / False

4. 놀부가 박을 잘랐을 때 보물이 나왔다. ————————— True / False

5. 흥부는 부자가 되었다. —————————————————— True / False

Modern Application

> "Heungbu and Nolbu" is one of the most well-known Korean folktales, so most Koreans are familiar with its plot and characters.
>
> In particular, the character "Nolbu" is most frequently mentioned, and you can say " casual 놀부 같다. (= The person is just like Nolbu.)", " casual 네가 놀부도 아니고. (= You're not Nolbu or something.)" when referring to someone who is jealous, greedy, or stingy. This type of characteristic is also referred to as "놀부 심보 (= Nolbu-like state of mind)", which can be expressed in sentences like " casual 무슨 놀부 심보야? (= What kind of Nolbu-like behavior is that?)" or " casual 놀부 심보가 따로 없다. (= That's exactly the kind of thing Nolbu would do.)"
>
> Example Dialogue (1)   🎧 Track 20
>
> 도윤: 이것 좀 봐. 나 이 신발 반값에 샀다! 5만 원에 샀어.
>
> 다혜: 와, 진짜 싸다! 참, 이 신발 예지도 사고 싶다고 했는데. 예지한테도 알려 주자.

도윤: 다른 애들한테는 말하지 마. 그럼 내가 할인받은 기분이 안 나잖아.

다혜: 뭐라고? 놀부 심보가 따로 없다, 정말.

Doyun: Look at these. I bought these shoes at half price! I got them
for 50,000 won.

Dahye: Wow, that's really cheap! By the way, Yeji said she wants
to buy these shoes too. Let's tell her.

Doyun: Don't tell other people. Otherwise, I won't feel like I got a
good deal.

Dahye: What? You're acting just like Nolbu, seriously.

Example Dialogue (2)

엄마: 아들, 동생한테도 과자 하나 줘야지.

아들: 싫어요! 저만 먹을 거예요!

엄마: 같이 먹으라고 사 준 건데 놀부처럼 그러면 안 되지!

Mother: Son, you should give your younger sibling a snack too.

Son: I don't want to! I'm going to eat it all by myself!

Mother: I bought it for both of you to share. You shouldn't act like
Nolbu!

Answers

1. True 2. False 3. True 4. False 5. True

11

How to Become an Actual Cow-boy

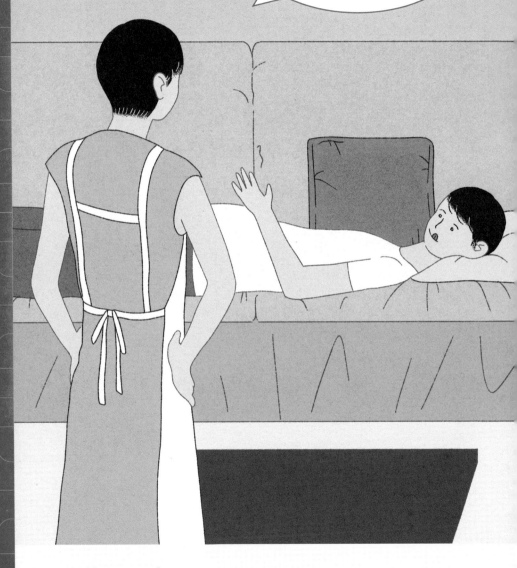

How come?
Find out on the next page

소가 된 게으름뱅이

옛날 어느 마을에 일하기 싫어하는 게으름뱅이가 살고 있었어요. 게으름뱅이의 부인은 하루 종일 잠만 자는 남편이 한심했어요.

"여보, 당신도 나가서 일 좀 해요. 일을 해야 우리도 먹고살죠."

하지만 게으름뱅이는 부인의 말을 듣지 않았어요.

어느 날, 게으름뱅이가 평소처럼 밥을 먹고 낮잠을 자고 있었어요.

"여보! 좀 일어나 봐요. 언제까지 이렇게 먹고 자기만 할 거예요?"

부인의 잔소리가 듣기 싫었던 게으름뱅이는 집을 나갔어요.

집을 나간 게으름뱅이는 그늘에서 풀을 뜯어 먹고 있던 소를 보고 말했어요.

"저 소는 일도 안 하고 편하게 있네. 아, 나도 소가 된다면 얼마나 좋을까?"

그때 마침 게으름뱅이 앞을 지나가던 노인이 게으름뱅이에게 말을 걸었어요.

"소가 되고 싶다면 이 탈을 한번 써 봐. 이 탈을 쓰면 소가 될 수 있어."

"네? 정말이에요? 이 탈을 쓰면 소가 될 수 있다고요?"

게으름뱅이는 얼른 탈을 써 봤어요. '펑' 하는 소리가 나더니 게으름뱅이가 정말 소로 변했어요.

"와! 내가 정말 소가 됐네!"

게으름뱅이 `disapproving/casual` lazy person   종일 all day   한심하다 to be pathetic   여보 honey (to one's wife or husband)   당신 honey (to one's wife or husband)   먹고살다 to make a living   잔소리 nagging   그늘 shade   풀 grass   뜯다 to pluck   마침 just, just in time   탈 mask   얼른 immediately   펑 pop   와 wow

The Lazy Man Who Became a Cow

Once upon a time in a village, there lived a lazy man who hated to work. His wife found him pathetic because he would do nothing but sleep all day.

"Honey, you, too, should go out and work. You have to work so that we can make a living."

However, he did not listen to his wife.

One day, the lazy man was taking a nap as usual after having a meal.

"Honey! Please get up. Until when will you do nothing but eat and sleep like this?"

He left home because he did not want to hear his wife's nagging.

After he left home, the lazy man saw a cow grazing in the shade and said, "That cow is not working and looks comfortable. Oh! How nice would it be if I also became a cow?"

Just at that moment, an old man was passing in front of him and talked to him.

"If you want to become a cow, try this mask on. If you wear this mask, you can become a cow."

"What? Is that true? You are saying that I can become a cow if I wear this mask?"

He immediately tried the mask on. There was a popping sound, and he really turned into a cow.

"Wow! I have really become a cow!"

게으름뱅이는 이제부터 먹고 자기만 할 생각에 신났어요.

그런데 그때, 탈을 건네준 노인이 소가 된 게으름뱅이를 끌고 가기 시작했어요.

"이랴! 이놈의 소야, 얼른 가자."

"어? 할아버지, 어디 가는 거예요? 잠시만요!"

소가 된 게으름뱅이가 소리쳤어요. 하지만 소의 입에서 나오는 소리는 '음메' 하는 소
울음소리뿐이었어요.

시장에 도착한 노인은 소를 한 농부에게 팔았어요. 노인은 소를 농부에게 넘기며 말했어요.

"절대 이 소에게 무를 먹이지 마세요. 이 소는 무를 먹으면 죽습니다."

"그것 참 이상한 소네요."

"아니에요! 나는 소가 아니에요! 나는 사람이라고요!"

소가 된 게으름뱅이의 입에서는 여전히 '음메' 하는 소 울음소리만 나왔어요.

"이랴! 이랴! 더 빨리 움직이지 못해?"

그날 이후, 소가 된 게으름뱅이는 농부의 밭에서 하루 종일 일을 했어요.

"내가 게으름을 피우고 살아서 벌을 받은 거야. 아이고, 여보, 미안해."

게으름뱅이는 일하지 않고 놀기만 했던 지난날을 후회하고 반성했어요.

신나다 to be excited   건네주다 to hand over   끌다 to drag   이랴 giddy up   이놈 rascal
소리치다 to exclaim, to shout   음메 moo   울음소리 crying sound   농부 farmer   넘기다 to hand over
절대 never   참 very   여전히 still   밭 field   게으름을 피우다 to be lazy   벌 punishment   아이고 jeez
지난날 the past days   후회하다 to regret   반성하다 to reflect on (in self-examination)

He was excited at the thought of doing nothing but eating and sleeping from then on.

At that moment, however, the old man, who had handed him the mask, started to drag the lazy man who was now a cow.

"Giddy up! You rascal, hurry and go."

"Huh? Old man, where are we going? Just a minute!"

The man-turned-cow exclaimed. However, the only sound that came out of his mouth was "moo".

The old man arrived at the market and sold the cow to a farmer. As he was handing him over to the farmer, he said, "Do not ever feed this cow radishes. It will die if it eats a radish."

"That is such a weird cow."

"No! I am not a cow! I am a human!"

Still, "moo" was the only thing coming out of the lazy man's mouth.

"Giddy up! Giddy up! Can you not move faster?"

From that day forward, the lazy man who became a cow worked all day long in the farmer's fields.

"I was punished because I was being lazy. Jeez... honey, I am sorry."

He was filled with regret and reflected back on the past when he only lazed away and did not work.

소가 된 게으름뱅이

그러던 어느 날, 소가 된 게으름뱅이가 힘들게 일을 하다가 무밭을 보게 됐어요. 그리고 무를 먹으면 죽는다고 한 노인의 말이 생각났어요.

'더 이상 이렇게 힘들게 살 수는 없어! 차라리 무를 먹고 죽는 게 낫겠어.'

게으름뱅이는 무를 하나 뽑아 먹었어요.

그때, 펑 소리가 나더니 신기한 일이 벌어졌어요. 게으름뱅이가 다시 사람의 모습으로 변했어요. 알고 보니 무를 먹으면 죽는 게 아니었어요. 다시 사람으로 변하는 거였어요. 노인이 거짓말을 한 거예요.

"와! 내가 다시 사람이 됐어!"

다시 사람이 된 게으름뱅이는 너무 기뻐 소리쳤어요.

게으름뱅이는 바로 집으로 돌아가 부인에게 그동안 있었던 일을 말했어요. 그리고 그 후로 게으름뱅이는 누구보다 더 열심히 일하는 부지런한 사람이 되었어요.

무밭 radish field 차라리 rather 신기하다 to be marvellous 벌어지다 to happen

And then one day, the lazy man who became a cow happened to see a radish field while he was toiling away. He remembered the old man saying that he will die if he eats a radish.

"I cannot live a hard life like this anymore! I would rather eat a radish and die."

The lazy man pulled out a radish and ate it.

Then there was a popping sound, and something marvelous happened. The lazy man turned back into human form. It was not that he would die if he ate a radish. It was that he would turn back into a human. The old man had lied.

"Wow! I have become human again!"

The lazy man who became human again exclaimed in delight.

The lazy man returned home right away and told his wife about what had happened to him during that time. After that, he became a diligent person who worked harder than anyone else.

Comprehension Quiz

Read the statements below and mark them as true or false.

1. 게으름뱅이는 탈을 쓰고 난 뒤 소로 변했다. ———————— True / False
2. 노인은 소가 된 게으름뱅이를 농부에게 팔았다. ———————— True / False
3. 소가 된 게으름뱅이는 일을 하지 않고 놀기만 했다. ———————— True / False
4. 노인은 거짓말을 했다. ———————— True / False
5. 소가 된 게으름뱅이는 풀을 먹고 다시 사람으로 변했다. ———————— True / False

Modern Application

When Korea was an agrarian society, cattle were essential for cultivation and were required to work hard all day long. The lazy man in the story, who didn't work at all, turned into an ox and worked very hard without rest. Therefore, this story gives the message, "Do what you have to do now, or you'll be forced to work even harder in the future."

You can quote this story to a person who is being lazy or idle. That's why parents in Korea often quote this story to their children. They believe lying down on a couch right after having a meal is not good for the stomach and makes people lazy, so they say " casual 그렇게 밥 먹고 바로 누우면 소 돼! (= If you lie down right after eating like that, you'll become a cow!)", as an idiomatic expression that means "Don't be a couch potato." or "Don't be so lazy."

🎧 Track 22

엄마: 밥 먹자마자 바로 누우면 어떡해?

아들: 딱 5분만요.

엄마: 그렇게 밥 먹고 바로 누우면 소 된다고 했지? 얼른 일어나.

Mom: How can you lie down right after having a meal?

Son: Just for five minutes.

Mom: I told you, you'll become a cow if you lie down right after
     eating like that! Hurry and get up.

Answers

1. True 2. True 3. False 4. True 5. False

12

Doppelganger Alert

How come?
Find out on the next page →

손톱 먹은 쥐

옛날 어느 마을에 한 부부가 살았어요. 부부에게는 아들이 하나 있었어요. 부부는 아들을 정말
사랑했어요. 그런데 아들은 부모님 말을 잘 듣지 않고, 공부도 열심히 하지 않았어요. 부부는
그런 아들이 너무 걱정됐어요.

"어휴, 우리 아들 좀 봐요. 하루 종일 놀기만 하네요."

"무슨 좋은 방법이 없을까요?"

"절로 보내는 게 어때요? 스님에게 이 아이를 엄격하게 가르쳐 달라고 부탁드려요."

"오, 좋은 생각이에요."

부부는 아들을 불러서 말했어요.

"아들아, 너를 절에 보내기로 했다. 3년만 절에서 지내도록 해라."

"네? 싫어요! 제가 왜요?"

아들은 절에 가기 싫어했어요.

"그럼 이렇게 계속 집에서 놀고먹기만 할 거야? 당장 가서 준비해!"

부부는 마음이 아팠지만 아들을 억지로 절로 보냈어요.

절에 도착한 아들은 허름한 절을 보고 말했어요.

"아이고. 이런 곳에서 어떻게 살아."

아들은 빨리 집으로 돌아가고 싶었어요.

손톱 fingernail 쥐 mouse 어휴 sound of sighing 종일 all day 절 temple 스님 honorific Buddhist
monk 엄격하다 to be strict 오 oh 놀고먹다 to live idle, to do nothing but play and eat 당장 right now
억지로 forcefully 허름하다 to be shabby 아이고 jeez

The Mouse That Ate Fingernails

Once upon a time in a village, there lived a married couple. The couple had a son. They loved their son very much. However, the son did not listen to his parents and did not study hard. The couple was very worried about their son.

"Sigh, look at our son. He just plays all day long."

"Is there any good solution?"

"How about sending him to a temple? Let us ask a monk to teach him strictly."

"Oh, that is a good idea."

The couple called their son and said, "Son, we have decided to send you to a temple. Stay there for just three years."

"What? I do not want to! Why should I?"

The son did not want to go to the temple.

"Then, will you just keep slacking at home? Go get ready right now!"

The couple's hearts were aching, but they forced their son to go to the temple.

When the son arrived at the temple, he looked at the shabby temple and said,

"Jeez, how can I live in a place like this?"

The son wanted to go back home as soon as possible.

손톱 먹은 쥐

한숨을 쉬고 있는 아들에게 한 스님이 다가왔어요.

"잘 왔다. 저기가 앞으로 네가 지낼 방이야. 일단 얼른 씻고 오렴. 그 긴 손톱도 좀 자르고!"

"네."

아들은 씻고 나서 손톱을 깎았어요. 그리고 깎은 손톱을 마당에 휙 버리려고 했어요.

"이놈! 손톱을 함부로 버리면 안 되지! 그러다 큰일 나!"

"네..."

아들은 작은 목소리로 대답했어요.

"손톱을 잘 모아서 버린 다음, 얼른 가서 자라. 내일부터는 일찍 일어나서 일도 하고 공부도 해야 하니까."

"네? 네..."

아들은 더 작은 목소리로 대답했어요.

다음 날부터 아들은 일찍 일어나 일도 하고 공부도 하며 바쁘게 지냈어요. 일과 공부 모두 어렵고 힘들었지만, 아들은 조금씩 달라지고 있었어요.

어느 날 저녁, 아들이 공부를 마친 뒤 잠시 쉬고 있을 때였어요. 쥐 한 마리가 찍찍 소리를 내면서 아들에게 다가왔어요. 쥐는 아들을 가만히 바라보았어요. 그 모습이 신기했던 아들은 쥐에게 먹다가 남은 밥을 줬어요.

한숨을 쉬다 to sigh   다가오다 to approach, to come toward   얼른 quickly   휙 quickly   이놈 rascal

함부로 carelessly   큰일 big trouble   달라지다 to change   찍찍 squeak   가만히 motionlessly

신기하다 to find something intriguing

As the son was sighing, a monk approached him.

"Welcome. That over there is the room where you will stay from now on. First, go and take a quick shower. Also, trim those long nails!"

"Okay."

After the son took a shower, he trimmed his nails. Then, he was about to quickly throw away the trimmed nails in the yard.

"You rascal! You should not throw away your nails carelessly! That can cause big trouble!"

"Okay..."

The son replied in a small voice.

"After gathering the trimmed nails properly and throwing them away, hurry up and go get some sleep. Starting from tomorrow, you have to wake up early, work, and study."

"Pardon? Okay..."

The son replied in a smaller voice.

From the next day on, the son woke up early, worked, and studied, keeping himself busy. Both work and study were difficult and challenging, but the son was gradually changing.

One evening, while the son was taking a break after finishing his studies, a mouse approached him, making squeaking noises. The mouse kept staring at the son. Intrigued by the scene, he gave the mouse some leftover food to eat.

그 후에도 쥐는 저녁이 되면 아들을 찾아왔어요. 아들은 쥐가 점점 편해졌어요. 아들은 쥐에게
자기 이야기를 하기 시작했어요.

"난 어서 빨리 집에 가고 싶어."

그럴 때마다 쥐는 마치 아들의 이야기를 알아듣는 것처럼 아들을 바라보며 옆에 있었어요.

집에 가고 싶다는 생각을 하면 할수록, 아들은 일과 공부가 하기 싫어졌어요. 아들은 점점
스님이 볼 때만 청소하거나 공부하고 스님 말도 잘 안 듣기 시작했어요.

"얘야, 깎은 손톱과 발톱을 잘 정리해서 버리라고 했지?"

"저녁에 정리하려고 했어요!"

"어휴, 저 애가 다시 예전처럼 게을러졌구나."

스님은 그런 아들을 보고 한숨을 쉬곤 했어요.

어느덧 3년이 흘러, 아들이 집에 돌아갈 때가 됐어요.

"와! 드디어 내일이면 집에 가는구나!"

아들은 신나서 짐을 싸고, 깨끗하게 목욕도 했어요. 그리고 마지막으로 손톱도 깎았어요.

"어휴, 귀찮아."

손톱을 함부로 버리지 말라고 한 스님의 말이 생각났지만, 귀찮았던 아들은 깎은 손톱을 마당에
던져 버렸어요.

"에잇, 마지막인데 뭐 어때?"

알아듣다 to understand 애 hey, kid 예전 the past 어느덧 before one knows 흐르다 to flow, to pass
와 wow 신나다 to be excited 에잇 sound that someone makes when they knowingly make a careless
decision

From that day on, the mouse would come to the son when evening came. The son
became more comfortable with the mouse. He started telling the mouse about himself.
"I really want to go home quickly."
Every time he said that, the mouse would look at him as if it was understanding his
words and stayed by his side.

The more he thought about going home, the more he grew reluctant to work and study.
He began to clean or study only when the monk was watching and started ignoring the
monk's instructions.
"Hey, didn't I tell you to throw away the trimmed nails and toenails in a tidy manner?"
"I was going to do it in the evening!"
"Sigh, that kid has become lazy again like before."
The monk would sigh when he saw the son behaving like that.

Before he knew it, three years passed, and it was time for the son to return home.
"Wow! Finally, tomorrow I will be going home!"
The son packed his belongings in excitement and took a clean bath as well. And finally,
he trimmed his nails one last time.
"Sigh, it is such a bother."
He remembered the monk's words not to throw away the trimmed nails carelessly, but
he found it bothersome and threw the trimmed nails into the yard.
"Well, it is the last time anyway. Who cares?"

손톱 먹은 쥐

그리고 다음 날, 아들은 아침이 되자마자 집으로 갔어요.

"어머니! 아버지! 저 왔어요!"

그런데 그때였어요.

"너 누구야?"

아들과 똑같이 생긴 아이가 아들을 향해 말했어요. 아들은 깜짝 놀랐어요.

"나? 나 이 집 아들이지! 넌 누구야?"

"무슨 소리야! 내가 이 집 아들인데!"

"뭐라고? 거짓말하지 마. 내가 진짜 이 집 아들이야."

"아니야! 내가 진짜야!"

두 아이는 결국 싸우기 시작했어요. 안에 있던 부부가 놀라서 밖으로 뛰어나왔어요.

"세상에! 이게 무슨 일이야?"

부부는 두 아들을 번갈아 쳐다보았어요. 얼굴도 목소리도, 심지어 몸에 있는 작은 점까지도 모두 똑같았어요.

결국 부부는 아이들을 데리고 원님을 찾아갔어요. 원님은 진짜 아들을 찾기 위해 이렇게 물어봤어요.

"부모님의 생신이 언제인지 말해 봐라."

진짜 아들은 바로 대답하려고 했지만 당황해서 잘 기억이 나지 않았어요.

"아버지 생신은 3월..."

진짜 아들이 더듬거리자 가짜 아들이 재빨리 말했어요.

향하다 to face 결국 eventually 뛰어나오다 to rush out 세상에 oh my 번갈아 in turn, back and forth
심지어 even 점 dot, mole 데리다 to take/bring someone 원님 honorific wonnim, term used to
address a local governor in the Joseon Dynasty 당황하다 to be flustered 더듬거리다 to stutter
재빨리 quickly

And the next day, as soon as morning came, the son went home.

"Mother! Father! I am back!"

But at that moment... "Who are you?"

A child who looked exactly like the son spoke to him. The son was astonished.

"Me? I am the son of this family! Who are you?"

"What are you talking about? I am the son of this family!"

"What? Do not lie. I am the real son of this family."

"No! I am the real one!"

The two children eventually started fighting. The parents, who were inside, were shocked and rushed out.

"Oh my! What is going on?"

The parents looked back and forth between the two sons. Their faces, voices, and even the small moles on their bodies were all the same.

In the end, the parents took the children and went to *wonnim*. Wonnim asked them like this in order to find the real son.

"Tell me when your parents' birthdays are."

The real son tried to answer immediately but became flustered and could not remember well.

"Father's birthday is in March..."

As the real son stuttered, the fake son quickly spoke up.

"아버지 생신은 8월 5일이고, 어머니 생신은 2월 15일입니다."
가짜 아들이 진짜 아들보다 더 대답을 잘했어요.
"네가 진짜 아들이구나! 가짜 아들에게 벌을 주어라!"

진짜 아들은 매를 맞고 쫓겨나 길에서 울기 시작했어요. 아들은 그동안의 일들이 다
후회됐어요.
"부모님 생신도 기억하지 못하다니, 난 나쁜 아들이야. 흑흑. 이제 어디로 가야 하지?"
그때 갑자기 스님의 얼굴이 떠올랐어요. 아들은 다시 절로 갔어요. 아들은 눈물을 흘리며
스님에게 집에서 있었던 일을 다 이야기했어요. 스님은 아들의 이야기를 듣더니 한 가지 방법을
알려 줬어요.
"고양이를 숨기고 집으로 가서 가짜 아들 앞에서 고양이를 꺼내 보아라."

아들은 근처에서 고양이를 찾았어요. 그리고 그 고양이를 옷 속에 숨겨서 집으로 갔어요.
"너 이놈!"
부부는 진짜 아들을 보고 소리를 질렀어요. 그 소리를 듣고 가짜 아들이 방에서 나와 말했어요.
"아버지, 어머니, 저 가짜를 얼른 내쫓아요!"

벌 punishment   매 rod   맞다 to be hit, to be beaten   쫓겨나다 to be kicked out   후회하다 to regret
흑흑 sound of sobbing   떠오르다 to strike, to occur to   눈물을 흘리다 to shed tears   숨기다 to hide
내쫓다 to kick out

"Father's birthday is August 5th, and mother's birthday is February 15th."
The fake son answered better than the real son.
"So you are the real son! Punish the fake son!"

The real son was beaten and kicked out, so he started crying on the street. He
regretted everything that had happened.
"Forgetting even my parents' birthdays, I am a bad son. Sob, sob. Where should I go
now?"
At that moment, the face of the monk came to his mind. The son went back to the
temple. With tears streaming down his face, he told the monk everything that had
happened at home. The monk listened to the son's story and taught him one method.
"Go back home with a hidden cat. Then, reveal the cat in front of the fake son."

The son found a cat nearby. He hid the cat in his clothes and went back home.
"You rascal!"
The parents shouted when they saw the real son. Hearing the sound, the fake son
came out of the room and said, "Father, mother, quickly kick out that imposter!"

손톱 먹은 쥐

그때 진짜 아들이 옷 속에서 고양이를 꺼냈어요. 고양이는 바로 가짜 아들에게 달려갔어요.
그러자 놀라운 일이 생겼어요. '펑' 하는 소리와 함께 가짜 아들이 쥐로 변한 거예요. 그 모습을
본 부부는 깜짝 놀라 진짜 아들에게 달려갔어요.
"아이고, 네가 진짜 아들이구나!"
"어머니, 아버지!"
부부와 아들은 서로 안고 눈물을 흘렸어요.

며칠 뒤, 부부와 아들은 스님을 찾아갔어요.
"스님, 정말 감사합니다. 그런데 스님은 고양이를 데리고 가면 된다는 걸 어떻게 아셨나요?"
스님이 웃으며 말했어요.
"오래 산 동물들은 사람의 손톱이나 발톱을 먹고 그 사람으로 변할 수 있지요. 이 아이가 마당에
버린 손톱을 먹고 쥐가 사람으로 변한 거예요. 얘야, 그러게 내가 손톱을 잘 모아서 버리라고
했지?"
아들은 자기 행동을 크게 반성했어요. 그 뒤로 아들은 새로운 사람이 되었어요. 공부도 열심히
하고 게으름도 피우지 않았어요. 그리고 부모님 말도 잘 들어서 마을에서 늘 칭찬을 받았다고
해요.

달려가다 to run   펑 pop   그러게 I told you so   반성하다 to reflect on (in self-examination)
게으름을 피우다 to be lazy

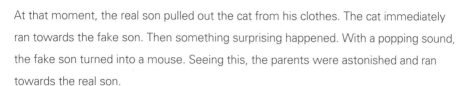

At that moment, the real son pulled out the cat from his clothes. The cat immediately ran towards the fake son. Then something surprising happened. With a popping sound, the fake son turned into a mouse. Seeing this, the parents were astonished and ran towards the real son.

"Jeez, you are the real son!"

"Mother, father!"

The parents and son embraced each other, shedding tears.

A few days later, the parents and son went to the monk.

"Monk, thank you so much. But how did you know that bringing a cat would work?"

The monk smiled and said, "Animals that have lived for a long time can consume human fingernails or toenails and transform into that person. The mouse ate the fingernails that this child threw in the courtyard, and turned into a human. Hey, I told you to gather and dispose of the nails properly, didn't I?"

The son deeply reflected on his actions. From then on, he became a new person. He studied hard and avoided laziness. Also, it is said that he listened well to his parents, so he always received praise from the villagers.

Comprehension Quiz

Read the statements below and mark them as true or false.

1. 아들은 항상 공부를 열심히 했다. ⋯⋯⋯⋯⋯⋯⋯⋯⋯⋯⋯⋯⋯ True / False

2. 아들은 3년 동안 절에 있었다. ⋯⋯⋯⋯⋯⋯⋯⋯⋯⋯⋯⋯⋯ True / False

3. 진짜 아들과 가짜 아들의 목소리는 달랐다. ⋯⋯⋯⋯⋯⋯⋯⋯ True / False

4. 원님 덕분에 진짜 아들을 찾을 수 있었다. ⋯⋯⋯⋯⋯⋯⋯⋯ True / False

5. 쥐가 아들의 손톱을 먹고 사람으로 변했다. ⋯⋯⋯⋯⋯⋯⋯⋯ True / False

Modern Application

In the Joseon Dynasty, people believed that they should cherish the body that they inherited from their parents. They even took care to dispose of their fingernails and toenails properly, believing that those body parts should be treated with great care. This belief was reflected in the story, which teaches us the lesson that we should take care of what we inherit from our parents.

Another lesson from this story is the importance of diligence and cleanliness. Korean parents often use the story to teach their children to be careful with their nails and dispose of them properly, using phrases like " casual 손톱 자르고 잘 모아서 버려. (= Gather your nails after cutting and dispose of them properly.)" or " casual 손톱 함부로 버리면 쥐가 손톱 먹고 너로 변한다! (= If you throw your nails away carelessly, a mouse will eat them and turn into you!)"

In this story, the mouse that ate fingernails becomes the same person as the son and tries to kick him out of the house. This is why people jokingly say, "현우 씨 손톱 먹은 쥐 같아요. (= He/She looks like a mouse that ate Hyunwoo's fingernails.)" when seeing someone who looks very similar to someone else.

Example Dialogue (1)　　　　　　　　　　　　　　　　 Track 24

　경화: 제발 손톱 좀 잘 모아서 버려 줄래? 지난번에도 내가 네 손톱 밟았단
　　　　 말이야. 쥐가 네 손톱 먹으면 어쩌려고 그래?

　민호: 오히려 좋아. 누가 내 손톱 먹고 나 대신 회사 가 줬으면 좋겠다.

　경화: 어휴.

　Kyung-hwa: Can you please gather and dispose of your nails
　　　　　　　 properly? I stepped on your nail last time, too. What
　　　　　　　 would you do if a mouse eats your fingernails?

　Minho: I'd actually like that. I wish someone would eat my
　　　　　 fingernails and go to work instead of me.

　Kyung-hwa: Sigh.

Example Dialogue (2)

　경은: 현우 씨, 왜 이렇게 일찍 출근했어요?

　현우: 이제부터 일찍 다닐 거예요.

　경은: 진짜 현우 씨 맞아요? 현우 씨 손톱 먹은 쥐 아니에요?

　현우: 하하. 진짜 저 맞아요.

　Kyeong-eun: Hyunwoo, why did you come to work so early?

　Hyunwoo: From now on, I'll be coming early.

　Kyeong-eun: Are you really Hyunwoo? Aren't you a mouse that ate
　　　　　　　 Hyunwoo's fingernails?

　Hyunwoo: Haha. It's really me.

Answers

1. False　2. True　3. False　4. False　5. True

13

A Huge Fan of Garlic

너 마늘 먹고 사람 돼야지!

You should eat garlic and become a human!

How come?
Find out on the next page

단군 이야기

아주 먼 옛날, 하늘 나라에 환인이라는 임금님이 살고 있었어요. 임금님에게는 환웅이라는
아들이 있었어요. 아들 환웅은 하늘 나라보다 인간 세상에 관심이 더 많았어요. 매일 인간
세상을 지켜보던 환웅은 인간 세상에 내려가 보고 싶었어요. 이런 아들의 마음을 알고 있었던
임금님이 환웅에게 말했어요.
"네가 인간 세상에 내려가 저곳을 더 아름답게 만들어 보아라."
"정말요? 감사합니다, 아버지!"
"그리고 하늘의 물건인 이 거울과 칼, 방울을 가져가도록 해라. 인간들이 네가 하늘에서 내려온
것을 알고 너를 섬길 것이다."

환웅은 3,000명의 신하와 임금님이 준 하늘의 물건을 가지고 인간 세상으로 내려갔어요. 신하
중에는 바람, 비, 그리고 구름을 다스리는 신하도 있었어요. 그렇게 환웅은 인간 세상을
다스리기 시작했어요.

그러던 어느 날이었어요. 환웅에게 곰 한 마리와 호랑이 한 마리가 찾아왔어요.
"환웅 님, 저희 좀 도와주세요."
"무슨 일이냐?"
"저희도 사람이 되고 싶습니다. 저희의 소원을 들어주세요."
"사람? 사람이 되는 건 쉬운 일이 아니다."

임금님 honorific king　인간 human　지켜보다 to observe　방울 bell　섬기다 to serve (king, god)
신하 servant, retainer, subject　다스리다 to govern, to rule　소원 wish　들어주다 to grant (one's wish)

일상 속에서 진짜 자주 등장하는 한국 옛날이야기

The Dan-gun Story

A very long time ago, in the heavenly kingdom, there lived a king named Hwanin. The king had a son named Hwanung. Hwanung was more interested in the human world than in the heavenly kingdom. Hwanung, who would observe the human world every day, wanted to go down to the human world. Aware of his son's desire, the king said to Hwanung.

"You shall go down to the human world and make it more beautiful."

"Really? Thank you, Father!"

"Also, take this mirror, sword, and bell, which are heavenly possessions. The humans will recognize that you have come from the heavens and serve you."

Hwanung descended to the human world with 3,000 servants and the heavenly possessions that the king had given him. Among his servants were those who controlled the wind, rain, and clouds. That is how Hwanung began to govern the human world.

Then one day, a bear and a tiger came to Hwanung.

"Hwanung, please help us."

"What is the matter?"

"We also want to become human. Please grant our wish."

"Human? To become human is not an easy task."

"저희도 알고 있습니다. 사람이 될 수만 있다면 무슨 일이든 하겠습니다."
호랑이와 곰의 간절한 부탁에 환웅은 쑥과 마늘을 주면서 말했어요.
"사람이 되려면 100일 동안 햇빛을 보지 않고, 이 쑥과 마늘만 먹으면서 지내야 한다. 할 수
있겠느냐?"
"네, 할 수 있습니다! 감사합니다, 환웅 님!"

그날부터 곰과 호랑이는 깜깜한 동굴에 들어가 쑥과 마늘만 먹기 시작했어요. 하지만 매일
그렇게 지내는 건 너무 어려웠어요. 동굴이 좁고 어두워서 곰과 호랑이는 너무 답답했어요. 쓴
쑥과 매운 마늘만 먹는 것도 너무 고통스러웠어요.

며칠이 지났을 때, 호랑이가 화를 내면서 곰에게 말했어요.
"에잇, 더 이상 쑥이랑 마늘을 못 먹겠어! 나는 당장 나갈래!"
곰은 호랑이를 달래며 말했어요.
"조금만 더 있으면 우리도 사람이 될 수 있어. 나랑 같이 조금만 더 견디자."
"에잇, 몰라! 난 그냥 나가서 맛있는 고기 먹을래!"
호랑이는 그렇게 말하고는 동굴 밖으로 뛰쳐나가 버렸어요. 혼자 남은 곰은 더 외롭고
힘들었지만, 사람이 될 날을 기다리면서 참고 견뎠어요.

곰이 동굴에서 혼자 쑥과 마늘만 먹은 지 21일째가 되던 날이었어요. 갑자기 동굴 안에서 환한
빛이 나더니 곰이 아름다운 여자로 변했어요.

간절하다 to be earnest 쑥 mugwort 마늘 garlic 깜깜하다 to be very dark 동굴 cave 고통스럽다 to be
agonizing 에잇 sound that someone makes when they knowingly make a careless decision 당장 right
now 달래다 to calm, to comfort 견디다 to endure 뛰쳐나가다 to dash out 환하다 to be bright

일상 속에서 진짜 자주 등장하는 한국 옛날이야기

"We are also aware of that. We will do anything if we can become human."

Since the tiger and the bear made their request earnestly, Hwanung handed them mugwort and garlic and said, "To become human, you must live for 100 days without seeing sunlight, only eating mugwort and garlic. Can you do it?"

"Yes, we can! Thank you, Hwanung!"

From that day on, the bear and the tiger entered a very dark cave and began eating only mugwort and garlic. However, living like that every day was extremely challenging. The cave was narrow and dark, making the bear and the tiger feel frustrated. Eating only bitter mugwort and spicy garlic was also too painful.

After a few days, the tiger became angry and said to the bear, "Well, I cannot eat mugwort and garlic anymore! I am going out right now!"

The bear appealed to the tiger and said, "If we stay just a little longer, we can become human, too. Let us endure a little more together."

"Well, I do not care! I am just going to go out and eat delicious meat!" replied the tiger, and he ended up dashing out of the cave. Left alone, the bear felt even lonelier and had a more difficult time, but he persevered, waiting for the day to become human.

It was the 21st day since the bear had been eating only mugwort and garlic alone in the cave. Suddenly, a bright light shone from inside the cave, and the bear transformed into a beautiful woman.

곰은 아직 100일이 되지 않았는데 사람이 된 것이 믿기지 않았어요. 그때 사람이 된 곰 앞에 환웅이 나타났어요. 환웅이 약속을 잘 지키고 있는 곰이 대견해서 약속한 시간보다 빨리 사람으로 변하게 해 준 거예요.

"세상에, 내가 정말로 사람이 됐구나! 정말 감사합니다, 환웅 님!"

곰은 감격해서 말했어요.

사람들은 여자가 된 곰을 웅녀라고 불렀어요. 웅녀는 다른 사람들처럼 결혼하고 아이를 갖고 싶었어요. 하지만 곰이었던 웅녀와 결혼하고 싶어 하는 사람은 없었어요. 그래서 웅녀는 매일 하늘에 기도했어요.

"흑흑. 저도 결혼을 하고 아이를 갖고 싶습니다. 제발 저의 소원을 들어주세요."

비가 오는 날에도, 눈이 오는 날에도 웅녀는 간절히 기도했어요. 그 모습을 본 환웅은 정성을 다하는 웅녀의 모습에 감동했어요. 그래서 환웅은 이번에도 웅녀의 소원을 들어주기로 했어요. 환웅은 인간 남자의 모습으로 변해 웅녀와 결혼했어요.

곧 웅녀는 원하던 대로 아이를 가졌어요. 시간이 흘러 아이는 아주 우렁찬 소리를 내면서 태어났어요.

"아가야, 훌륭하게 자라렴."

훗날 아이는 웅녀의 바람대로 훌륭하게 자라 나라를 세웠어요. 그 나라가 한국 최초의 국가 '고조선'이고, 그가 바로 '단군왕검'이에요.

대견하다 to be proud   세상에 oh my   정말로 truly   감격하다 to be deeply moved   기도하다 to pray
흑흑 sound of sobbing   정성 devotion, one's heart   감동하다 to be touched   시간이 흐르다 time passes
우렁차다 to be loud and powerful   아가 word used to address a baby   훗날 some day   바람 wish
최초 the first   고조선 *Gojoseon*, the name of the first nation of Korea

The bear could not believe that she had become human even though it had not been 100 days yet. At that moment, Hwanung appeared in front of the bear who had become human. Hwanung was impressed by the bear's dedication in keeping the promise and granted her the transformation into a human earlier than the agreed-upon time.

"Oh my, I have truly become a human! Thank you so much, Hwanung!" said the bear, deeply moved.

People called the bear-turned-woman "Ungnyeo". Ungnyeo wanted to get married and have children like other people. However, no one wanted to marry Ungnyeo, who used to be a bear. So Ungnyeo prayed to the heavens every day.

"Sob, I also want to get married and have children. Please grant my wish."

Even on rainy days and snowy days, Ungnyeo prayed fervently. Witnessing Ungnyeo's heartfelt devotion, Hwanung was touched. Therefore, Hwanung decided to grant Ungnyeo's wish this time as well. He transformed into a human man and married Ungnyeo.

Soon, Ungnyeo had a child as she wanted. As time passed, the child was born with a loud and powerful sound.

"My child, may you grow up splendidly."

In the future, the child grew up well, just as Ungnyeo wished, and established a country. That country is the first nation of Korea, called "*Gojoseon*", and the child is none other than "Dan-gun Wanggeom".

Comprehension Quiz

Read the statements below and mark them as true or false.

1. 환웅은 인간 세상에 관심이 없었다. ⸻ True / False

2. 환웅은 곰과 호랑이에게 100일 동안
   동굴에서 쑥과 마늘만 먹으라고 했다. ⸻ True / False

3. 호랑이는 남자가 되었다. ⸻ True / False

4. 곰은 여자가 되었다. ⸻ True / False

5. 웅녀와 환웅의 아들이 단군왕검이다. ⸻ True / False

Modern Application

The Dan-gun story is the founding myth of Korea, so it's well-known among Koreans. That's why in Korea, you often see some brand names such as 단군 떡볶이 (= Dan-gun tteokbokki) or 단군 태권도 (= Dan-gun taekwondo), named after the very first king of Korea, Dan-gun Wanggeom. There is a national holiday associated with this story: 개천절 (Gaecheonjeol). 개천절 is the national foundation day of Korea, meaning that the beginning of the country was by those who descended from the heaven and is celebrated on October 3rd annually.

While reading the story, you might wonder why it was a bear that actually became a human. It actually represents the culture of worship of bears at that time. In this story, the part where the bear eats garlic and mugwort is quoted a lot. It can be used as " casual 마늘이랑 쑥 먹고 사람 돼야지. (= You should become human by eating garlic and mugwort.)" or " casual 마늘 먹고 사람 좀

돼라. (= Eat garlic and be a human.)" and "becoming human" in these phrases is an idiomatic expression that means "to behave well" or "to function properly as a human being". Garlic is used more prominently in these expressions because Koreans consume much more garlic than mugwort in daily life. The actual meaning of the expression isn't about becoming a literal human being, but rather becoming a morally mature person. So you can use this to someone who behaves recklessly or immaturely.

Example Dialogue

🎧 Track 26

도윤: 고기 굽게?

은경: 응. 너도 먹을 거지?

도윤: 응. 근데 마늘이 왜 이렇게 많아? 고기 반 마늘 반이네.

은경: 우리 도윤이 마늘 먹고 사람 돼야지!

도윤: 됐거든? 나는 그냥 호랑이 할래.

Doyun: Are you going to grill some meat?

Eunkyeong: Yeah. You're going to eat, too, right?

Doyun: Yeah. But why do we have so much garlic? It's half meat, half garlic.

Eunkyeong: My dear Doyun should eat garlic and become a human!

Doyun: Whatever! I'll just be a tiger.

Answers

1. False 2. True 3. False 4. True 5. True

14

Someone Is in My House!

How come?
Find out on the next page

우렁이 각시

옛날에 착하고 성실한 남자가 있었어요. 어느 날, 논에서 열심히 일을 하던 남자가 혼잣말을
했어요.

"어휴, 힘들다. 그냥 집에 갈까? 아니야. 집에 가도 아무도 없어서 외롭기만 하지."

그러자 누군가 작은 목소리로 말했어요.

"나랑 살자!"

남자는 놀라서 주변을 둘러봤지만 아무도 없었어요. 남자는 잘못 들었다고 생각하고 다시
일하기 시작했어요.

일을 다 끝낸 남자는 또 혼잣말을 했어요.

"어휴, 이렇게 열심히 일해서 뭐 해. 이걸 같이 먹을 사람도 없는데!"

"나랑 같이 먹자!"

작은 목소리가 또 들렸어요. 남자가 주변을 다시 둘러보니 커다란 우렁이 한 마리가 있었어요.

"이상하다. 여긴 우렁이밖에 없는데..."

그 우렁이는 남자가 지금까지 본 우렁이들보다 훨씬 컸어요. 남자는 커다란 우렁이가
신기하기도 하고 혼자 지내는 것이 외롭기도 해서 우렁이를 집에 가져갔어요. 그리고 가져간
우렁이를 큰 항아리 안에 넣어 두었어요.

우렁이 freshwater snail 각시 bride, wife 성실하다 to be diligent 논 rice paddy, field 혼잣말 talking to
oneself 어휴 sound of sighing 주변 surroundings 둘러보다 to look around 커다랗다 to be large
신기하다 to find something intriguing 항아리 traditional Korean earthenware jar

The Snail Bride

Once upon a time, there was a kindhearted and diligent man. One day, the man was working hard in a rice paddy and said to himself.

"Sigh, it is tough. Should I just go home? No, even if I go home, there is no one there, and I will just feel lonely."

Then, someone said in a small voice.

"Let us live together!"

The man was surprised and looked around, but there was no one there. He thought he must have misheard and started working again.

After finishing all of his work, the man said to himself again.

"Sigh, what is the point of working this hard? There is no one to eat this with!"

"Let us eat together!"

The small voice was heard again. When the man looked around again, there was a large freshwater snail.

"It is strange. There is only a snail here..."

That snail was much larger than any snail the man had seen before. The man was intrigued by the big snail and also felt lonely living by himself, so he took the snail home. And he put the snail in a large jar.

다음 날도 남자는 논에 가서 일을 하고 집에 돌아왔어요. 문을 열고 들어온 남자는 깜짝 놀랐어요. 맛있는 음식들이 준비되어 있고, 집도 깨끗하게 청소되어 있었어요.

"아니, 이게 무슨 일이지? 집에 올 사람이 없는데."

남자는 이상하다고 생각했지만 준비된 음식을 맛있게 먹었어요.

다음 날도, 그 다음 날도 일을 마치고 돌아오면 항상 맛있는 음식이 준비되어 있었어요. 남자는 기분이 좋았지만 조금 무섭기도 했어요.

'내일은 누가 다녀간 건지 꼭 알아내야겠어.'

다음 날, 남자는 일을 하러 가는 척하고 멀리 숨어서 집을 지켜봤어요. 잠시 후, 우렁이를 넣어 둔 항아리에서 밝은 빛이 나더니 한 여자가 항아리 밖으로 나왔어요. 남자는 믿을 수가 없었어요.

"이럴 수가! 항아리에서 사람이 나오다니!"

항아리에서 나온 여자는 정말 아름다웠어요. 남자는 여자에게 첫눈에 반했어요. 그 여자는 집을 깨끗하게 청소하고, 맛있는 음식을 만들었어요. 그리고 다시 항아리로 들어가려고 했어요.

남자는 얼른 뛰어가서 말했어요.

"잠시만요!"

여자는 남자를 보고 깜짝 놀랐어요.

"당신은 누구신가요? 왜 청소와 요리를 해 주시는 거예요?"

남자의 질문에 여자가 대답했어요.

알아내다 to find out   숨다 to hide   지켜보다 to observe   첫눈에 반하다 to fall in love at first sight

얼른 quickly   당신 honorific you

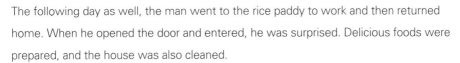

The following day as well, the man went to the rice paddy to work and then returned home. When he opened the door and entered, he was surprised. Delicious foods were prepared, and the house was also cleaned.

"Wow, what is going on? There is no one to come to my house."

The man thought it was strange but enjoyed the prepared meal.

The following day and the day after that, whenever the man finished his work and came back home, a delicious meal was always prepared. The man felt happy but also a little scared.

"Tomorrow, I am definitely going to find out who has been coming to my house."

The next day, the man pretended to go to work, but hid himself far away to observe his house. After a while, a bright light came out from the jar where the snail was kept, and a woman came out of it. The man could not believe it.

"No way! A person is coming out of the jar!"

The woman who came out from the jar was truly beautiful. The man fell in love with her at first sight. The woman cleaned the house and prepared a delicious meal. Then she tried to go back into the jar. The man quickly ran up to her and said,

"Wait!"

The woman was surprised to see the man.

"Who are you? Why are you cleaning and cooking for me?"

The woman responded to the man's question.

"며칠 전에 우렁이 한 마리를 이 항아리에 넣으셨죠? 제가 바로 그 우렁이예요. 저는 사실 바다 용왕님의 딸인데, 아버지 말씀을 듣지 않아서 벌을 받고 우렁이로 변하게 됐어요. 당신이 제 목소리를 듣고, 이 집으로 저를 데리고 와 줬어요. 당신에게 너무 고마워서 청소와 요리를 해 놓았어요. 저는 이제 며칠 뒤면 다시 사람이 돼요. 그동안 고마웠어요."

남자는 여자의 따뜻한 말을 듣고 감동했어요. 그리고 이렇게 마음이 따뜻한 사람과 살고 싶다는 생각을 했어요.

"저도 정말 고마워요. 당신 덕분에 며칠 동안 깨끗한 집에서 맛있는 음식을 먹을 수 있었어요. 당신처럼 마음이 따뜻한 사람과 함께하고 싶어요. 저와 결혼해 주시겠어요?"

여자도 진심을 다해서 말하는 남자가 싫지 않았어요.

그렇게 여자와 남자는 결혼해 행복한 하루하루를 보냈어요. 그러던 어느 날이었어요. 못되기로 소문난 원님이 마을을 지나가다가 여자를 보고 첫눈에 반했어요. 원님은 여자 옆에 남자가 있는 것을 보고 남자에게 물었어요.

"이 아름다운 여인은 누구냐?"

"이 여인은 제 아내입니다."

"뭐? 이렇게 아름다운 여인이 너같이 가난한 사람의 아내라고? 이 여인은 나와 사는 것이 좋겠다! 나와 내기를 하자! 내일 당장 뒷산으로 와라!"

원님은 내기에서 남자가 이기면 큰돈을 주고, 남자가 지면 아내를 데려가겠다고 했어요. 남자는 너무 억울했지만, 내기를 피할 수 없었어요.

용왕 the Dragon King 벌 punishment 감동하다 to be touched 함께하다 to be with 진심 one's heart, one's true feelings 하루하루 every day, from day to day 못되다 to be mean 소문나다 a rumor circulates, to be talked about 원님 honorific *wonnim*, term used to address a local governor in the Joseon Dynasty 여인 woman 가난하다 to be poor 내기 bet 뒷산 mountain behind one's house or town 큰돈 large sum of money 억울하다 to feel wronged 피하다 to avoid

일상 속에서 진짜 자주 등장하는 한국 옛날이야기

"A few days ago, you put a snail in this jar, right? I am that snail. I am actually the daughter of the Dragon King of the Sea, but I did not listen to my father's words and received a punishment, which turned me into a snail. You heard my voice and brought me to this house. I am so grateful to you, so I cleaned and cooked for you. In a few days, I will become human again. Thank you for everything."

The man was touched by the woman's warm words. And he thought he wanted to live with such a warm-hearted person.

"I am also really thankful. Thanks to you, I was able to eat delicious meal in a clean house for the past few days. I want to be with someone who is warm-hearted like you. Will you marry me?"

The woman also did not dislike the man, who spoke with full sincerity.

And just like that, the woman and the man got married and spent happy days together. And then one day, while *wonnim*, who was well-known for being mean, was passing through the village and saw the woman, fell in love at first sight. Wonnim noticed the man standing next to the woman and asked him, "Who is this beautiful woman?"

"This woman is my wife."

"What? This beautiful woman is the wife of someone as poor as you? It would be better if this woman lived with me! Let us make a bet! Come to the mountain behind the town tomorrow without delay!"

Wonnim suggested that if the man won a bet, he would give him a large sum of money, but if the man lost, he would take his wife away. The man felt this was very wrong, but he could not avoid taking the bet.

"어쩌면 좋습니까? 원님을 제가 어떻게 이길 수 있겠어요. 흑흑."

집으로 돌아온 남자는 눈물이 멈추지 않았어요. 그런 남자에게 여자는 손에 끼고 있던 반지를 건네주며 말했어요.

"저는 절대로 당신과 헤어지지 않을 거예요. 저에게 방법이 있으니 지금 바다에 가서 이 반지를 던지고 잠시 기다려 보세요."

남자는 곧바로 바다로 달려가 반지를 던졌어요. 그리고 놀라운 일이 벌어졌어요. 바닷속에서 용왕의 신하들이 나타나 남자를 용왕 앞으로 데리고 갔어요.

"원님이 제 아내를 데려가려고 합니다. 제발 도와주세요."

남자는 용왕에게 그동안 있었던 일을 모두 말했어요. 남자의 말을 들은 용왕은 작은 병 하나를 주면서 도움이 필요할 때마다 그 병을 열어 보라고 했어요.

다음 날, 남자는 병을 가지고 뒷산으로 갔어요.

"나무를 더 빨리 심는 사람이 이기는 것으로 하자!"

원님은 많은 신하를 데리고 나무를 심기 시작했어요. 원님과 신하들이 너무 빨라서 남자가 질 것 같았어요. 남자는 얼른 용왕이 준 병을 열었어요. 그러자 그 병 안에서 수많은 사람이 나와서 남자와 함께 나무를 심기 시작했어요. 덕분에 남자는 내기에서 쉽게 이길 수 있었어요. 하지만 못된 원님은 포기하지 않았어요.

흑흑 sound of sobbing   건네주다 to hand over   절대로 never   곧바로 immediately   벌어지다 to happen
바닷속 under the sea   신하 servant, retainer, subject   포기하다 to give up

"What should I do? How can I possibly defeat wonnim? Sob, sob."

The man came back home and could not stop his tears. To the man, who was feeling this way, the woman handed over the ring she had been wearing and said, "I will never leave you. I have a plan, so go to the sea now and throw this ring and wait for a while."

The man immediately ran to the sea and threw the ring. Then, something surprising happened. The Dragon King's servants emerged from the sea and took the man to the Dragon King.

"Wonnim is trying to take my wife away. Please help me."

The man told the Dragon King everything that had happened so far. Upon hearing the man's words, the Dragon King gave him a small bottle and told him to open it whenever he needed help.

The next day, the man took the bottle and went to the mountain behind the town.

"Let us make it a competition of who can plant trees faster!"

Wonnim brought many servants and started planting trees. Wonnim and his servants were so fast that the man thought he would lose. Quickly, the man opened the bottle the Dragon King had given him. Then, countless people emerged from the bottle and started planting trees with the man. Thanks to them, the man was able to easily win the bet. However, the mean wonnim would not give up.

"말도 안 돼! 이번에는 누가 말을 타고 더 빨리 달리는지 내기하자!"

원님에게는 아주 크고 좋은 말이 있었지만 남자는 말이 없었어요. 남자는 용왕이 준 병을
열었어요. 그러자 그 안에서 작고 마른 말 한 마리가 나왔어요.

'아이고. 이렇게 작고 마른 말로 원님을 이길 수 있을까?'

원님의 큰 말을 본 남자는 걱정됐어요. 하지만 내기가 시작되자 남자가 탄 작고 마른 말은
원님의 큰 말보다 훨씬 빠르게 달리기 시작했어요. 결국 남자가 또 원님을 이겼어요.

"정말 마지막으로 한 번 더 내기를 하자!"

두 번이나 진 것이 화가 난 원님은 다시 내기하자고 했어요. 이번에는 배를 타고 더 멀리 가는
사람이 이기는 내기를 하게 됐어요. 크고 멋진 원님의 배에 비해 남자의 배는 작고 초라했어요.
원님의 배가 남자의 배보다 훨씬 빠르게 가기 시작했어요. 남자는 이번에도 병을 열었어요.
그러자 신기한 일이 일어났어요. 갑자기 파도가 치기 시작하더니 파도가 원님의 배를 뒤집어
버렸어요.

바다에 빠져 죽을 뻔한 원님은 이제 남자와 내기하는 것이 무서워졌어요.

"내가 졌다."

원님은 여자를 데려오는 것을 포기하고, 약속했던 큰돈을 남자에게 주었어요. 용왕이 준 병
덕분에 내기에서 이긴 남자는 그렇게 부자가 되어 아내와 함께 오래오래 행복하게 살았다고
해요.

아이고 jeez 결국 in the end 초라하다 to be shabby, to be humble 파도 wave 치다 (wave) to crash
뒤집다 to overturn

"No way! Let us make a bet on who can ride a horse faster this time!"

Wonnim had a really big and good horse, but the man did not have a horse. The man opened the bottle the Dragon King had given him. Then, a small and skinny horse came out from it.

"Jeez. Can I beat wonnim with this small and skinny horse?"

The man was worried when he saw wonnim's big horse. However, as the bet started, the small, skinny horse the man was riding started running much faster than wonnim's big horse. In the end, the man beat wonnim again.

"Let us do one more bet for the very last time!"

Wonnim, angered by his two losses, suggested another bet. This time, they bet on who could sail farther on a boat. Compared to wonnim's boat which was grand and magnificent, the man's boat was small and shabby. Wonnim's boat started sailing much faster than the man's boat. This time as well, the man opened the bottle. Then, something mysterious happened. Suddenly, there were waves, which ended up overturning wonnim's boat.

Wonnim, who almost drowned in the sea, became scared of betting against the man.

"I lost."

Wonnim gave up on taking the woman and gave the man the large sum of money he had promised. The man, who won the bets thanks to the bottle the Dragon King had given him, became rich and lived happily ever after with his wife.

Comprehension Quiz

Read the statements below and mark them as true or false.

1. 남자는 우렁이를 항아리 안에 넣었다. ⸻⸻⸻ True / False
2. 남자가 집에 돌아왔을 때 집이 더러웠다. ⸻⸻⸻ True / False
3. 우렁이는 용왕의 딸이다. ⸻⸻⸻⸻⸻⸻ True / False
4. 남자는 원님하고 내기를 해서 모두 졌다. ⸻⸻ True / False
5. 원님은 우렁이와 결혼했다. ⸻⸻⸻⸻⸻ True / False

Modern Application

In this story, the snail sneaked into the man's house and did the cleaning and cooking. So, people often call someone who secretly does the household chores for others as 우렁 각시 (the snail bride). For example, when feeling too lazy to do household chores, you can say, "우렁 각시 어디 없나요? (= Is there any snail bride?)" or when a space unexpectedly becomes clean, you can say, " [casual] 우렁 각시가 왔다 갔나? (= Did the snail bride come and go?)"

Although 우렁이 is the standard term, Korean people tend to use the title of this story more often as 우렁 각시. Also, 각시 is an old-fashioned word for "bride", but in reality, the expression 우렁 각시 isn't limited to only women. People even transform this expression to 우렁 친구 (snail friend), 우렁 총각 (snail bachelor), or etc. instead of 우렁 각시.

Example Dialogue (1) Track 28

| (민지의 집에 놀러 온 준호)
| 준호: 오, 뭐야? 웬일로 집이 이렇게 깨끗해? 우렁 각시라도 왔다 갔어?

민지: 야, 나도 청소해야 할 땐 열심히 해.

준호: 거짓말하지 마. 네 방이 이렇게 깨끗한 건 처음 봐.

(Jun-ho visiting Minji's house)

Jun-ho: Oh, what's this? How come your house is this clean? Did the snail bride or someone come by?

Minji: Hey, when I need to clean, I do it diligently, too.

Jun-ho: Don't lie. I've never seen your room this clean before.

Example Dialogue (2)

다혜: 예림아, 우리 집 공사해야 하는데, 너희 집에서 일주일만 있어도 돼?

예림: 일주일이나?

다혜: 대신 내가 밥, 빨래 다 할게! 집에 우렁 친구 한 명 있다고 생각해.

예림: 어휴, 알겠어.

Dahye: Yerim, my house needs renovating. Can I stay at your place for just one week?

Yerim: One whole week?

Dahye: I'll take care of cooking and laundry in return! Just think of it as having a snail friend at home.

Yerim: Ugh, okay.

Answers

1. True 2. False 3. True 4. False 5. False

15

The Most Famous Name in Korea

내가 홍길동인 줄 아나 봐.

They think I'm Hong Gildong.

How come?

Find out on the next page

→

홍길동전

조선 시대에 홍길동이라는 남자아이가 살고 있었어요. 길동은 특별한 아이였어요. 어려서부터 똑똑하고 무술도 아주 잘했어요. 홍길동의 아버지는 그런 길동을 예뻐했어요. 홍길동의 아버지는 높은 벼슬을 가지고 있는 양반이었어요. 하지만 길동은 아버지와 달리, 양반이 될 수 없었어요. 길동은 아버지의 집에서 일하는 노비가 낳은 아들이었기 때문이에요. 길동은 양반의 아들로 인정받을 수 없었기 때문에 아버지를 아버지라고 부를 수 없었고, 아무리 무술을 잘해도 벼슬을 얻을 수도 없었어요.

어느 늦은 밤, 홍길동이 무술 연습을 하고 있었어요. 그 모습을 본 아버지가 물었어요.
"늦은 시간에 왜 여기서 이러고 있느냐?"
"마음이 갑갑해서 그렇습니다."
"무슨 일이 있었느냐?"
"아버지를 아버지라고, 형을 형이라고 부르지 못하는데 어떻게 갑갑하지 않을 수 있겠습니까?"
아버지는 마음이 너무 아팠어요. 하지만 길동을 위로했다가 길동이 자만하게 될까 봐 일부러 엄하게 말했어요.

-전 biography, life (story)　조선 시대 *Joseon Dynasty*, the name of the last dynastic kingdom of Korea (1392-1910)　남자아이 boy　무술 martial arts　벼슬 government position　양반 *yangban*, gentry of dynastic Korea during the Goryeo and Joseon Dynasties　노비 *nobi*, slave class during the Goryeo and Joseon Dynasties　인정 acknowledgment, recognition　갑갑하다 to feel frustrated 위로하다 to comfort　자만하다 to be big-headed, to be conceited　일부러 purposely　엄하다 to be strict, to be harsh

The Tale of Hong Gildong

In the *Joseon Dynasty*, there lived a boy named Hong Gildong. Gildong was a special child. From a young age, he was intelligent and good at martial arts. Gildong's father adored him for that. Gildong's father held a high position in society as a *yangban*. However, unlike his father, Gildong could not become a yangban. This was because he was born to a *nobi* working in his father's house. Since Gildong could not be recognized as a yangban's son, he could not address his father as "father", and no matter how skilled he was in martial arts, he could not obtain a government position.

One late night, Hong Gildong was practicing martial arts. His father, upon seeing him, asked, "Why are you doing this here at such a late hour?"
"Because I feel frustrated in my heart."
"What has happened?"
"I cannot call you 'father' or address my elder brother as 'brother'. How can I not feel frustrated?"
His father felt a great pain in his heart. However, fearing that comforting Gildong would make him arrogant, he purposely spoke sternly.

"어쩔 수 없다는 것을 잘 알지 않느냐? 다들 이렇게 살아간다. 괜한 소리 하지 말고, 어서
들어가서 자라."
홍길동은 아버지의 진심을 알고는 있었지만 너무 속상했어요.

그러던 어느 날이었어요. 길동이 잠을 자려고 누웠는데 문밖에서 작은 소리가 들렸어요. 길동은
안 좋은 느낌이 들어서 조용히 일어나 문 옆에 섰어요. 잠시 후 문이 열리더니 누군가 칼을 들고
방으로 들어왔어요. 길동은 재빨리 그 사람을 공격해서 칼을 빼앗았어요.
"넌 누구냐?"
알고 보니 그 사람은 아버지의 다른 부인이 보낸 사람이었어요. 자기 아들보다 훌륭한 홍길동을
미워해서 죽이려고 했던 거예요.

길동은 다음 날 아침 어머니를 찾아가 말했어요.
"어머니, 어젯밤에 누군가가 저를 죽이려고 했습니다. 저는 더 이상 이 집에서 살 수 없습니다.
제가 떠나야 어머니도 안전하실 거예요."
길동의 어머니는 너무 슬펐지만 길동을 잡을 수 없었어요.

집을 떠난 길동이 산속을 걷고 있었어요. 어디선가 사람들 소리가 들렸어요. 소리가 나는
곳으로 가 보니 도적들이 모여서 대장을 뽑고 있었어요.
"저 바위를 드는 사람이 우리의 대장이다!"

진심 one's heart, one's true feelings 속상하다 to be upset 재빨리 quickly 공격하다 to attack
빼앗다 to take, to extort 산속 inside the mountains 도적 thief 대장 leader 바위 rock

일상 속에서 진짜 자주 등장하는 한국 옛날이야기

"You know that there is nothing we can do about it. Everyone lives like this. Stop saying useless things and go inside and sleep."

Hong Gildong knew what his father's true feelings were, but he was deeply saddened.

Then, one day, as Gildong lay down to sleep, he heard a faint sound from outside the door. Gildong had a bad feeling, so he quietly got up and stood next to the door. After a moment, the door opened, and someone entered the room with a knife in hand. Gildong quickly attacked the person and took the knife away.

"Who are you?"

It turned out the person was sent by his father's other wife. She hated Gildong, who was better than her own son, so she tried to have him killed.

The next morning, Gildong went to his mother and said, "Mother, someone tried to kill me last night. I cannot live in this house any longer. You will only be safe if I leave."

Gildong's mother was very sad, but she could not stop him.

Gildong, who left home, was walking through the mountains. He could hear voices coming from somewhere. He followed the sound and discovered a group of thieves gathered, who were choosing their leader.

"The one who lifts that rock will be our leader!"

힘이라면 자신 있었던 홍길동이 당당하게 앞으로 나가 말했어요.

"저도 저 바위를 들어 보겠습니다."

도적들은 나이가 어려 보이는 길동을 무시했어요.

"하하, 여긴 너 같은 어린아이가 있을 곳이 아니야! 어서 집에나 가라."

그때였어요.

길동이 바위를 번쩍 들어 올렸어요.

"아니, 이럴 수가!"

이때까지 그 바위를 든 사람은 아무도 없었어요. 도적들은 홍길동에게 자기들의 대장이 되어

달라고 했어요. 그러자 길동은 이렇게 말했어요.

"좋습니다. 하지만 우리는 사람들을 도와주는 도적이 되어야 합니다. 양반들은 사람들을

괴롭혀서 더 부자가 되고, 가난한 사람들은 디 가난해지고 있습니다. 이런 양반들을 혼내 주고,

양반들이 빼앗은 것을 다시 사람들에게 돌려줍시다! 그리고 그것을 우리처럼 가난한 사람들과

함께 나눕시다."

도적들은 나이는 어리지만 지혜롭고 능력이 뛰어난 길동의 말을 듣기로 했어요.

"네, 대장님!"

그때부터 홍길동과 도적들은 나쁜 방법으로 부자가 된 사람들의 돈을 빼앗아 가난한

사람들에게 나누어 줬어요. 그리고 길동과 도적들은 자신들을 '활빈당'이라고 부르기

시작했어요.

당당하다 to be confident   무시하다 to look down on   하하 haha   번쩍 lightly, effortlessly

괴롭히다 to torment   가난하다 to be poor   혼내다 to scold   지혜롭다 to be wise   능력 ability

뛰어나다 to be exceptional

Confident in his strength, Hong Gildong stepped forward confidently and said, "I will try lifting that rock, too."

The thieves looked down on Gildong, who looked young.

"Haha, this is not a place for a little kid like you! Go home at once."

It was at that moment.

Gildong lifted the rock effortlessly.

"No way! How can this be?"

Until then, no one had been able to lift the rock. The thieves asked Gildong to become their leader. In response, Gildong said the following:

"Okay, but we must become thieves who help people. The yangbans are becoming richer by tormenting people, while the poor are becoming poorer. Let us confront these yangbans and return what they have taken from the people. And let us share it with poor people just like us."

The thieves decided to obey Gildong, who had wisdom and exceptional abilities despite being young.

"Yes, Captain!"

From then on, Hong Gildong and the thieves took money from the rich who had become rich through bad means and distributed it to the poor. And Gildong and the thieves began calling themselves the "Hwalbin" gang.

"우리는 활빈당이다! 가난한 사람들을 살린다는 뜻이다!"

"활빈당 만세!"

시간이 흐를수록 활빈당은 유명해졌고, 홍길동을 따르는 사람들도 점점 많아졌어요. 그러자 왕도 활빈당을 알게 되었어요.

"활빈당이 무엇이냐?"

왕이 신하들에게 물었어요. 나쁜 방법으로 부자가 된 양반들은 활빈당을 아주 싫어했어요. 그래서 거짓말을 했어요.

"활빈당은 착한 사람들의 돈을 훔치는 아주 못된 도적들입니다. 지금 당장 그들을 잡아야 합니다."

신하들의 말을 들은 왕이 말했어요.

"당장 활빈당을 잡아 와라! 특히 그 대장인 홍길동을 반드시 잡아 와라!"

신하들이 홍길동을 잡으려고 하자 홍길동은 마술을 부려서 자신과 똑같이 생긴 일곱 명의 가짜 홍길동을 만들었어요. 그렇게 여덟 명이 된 홍길동이 이곳저곳에서 보이자 신하들은 길동을 잡을 수가 없었어요. 사람들은 가짜 홍길동이 있는 줄도 모르고, 이곳저곳에서 보이는 홍길동을 보고 '동에서 번쩍하고, 서에서 번쩍한다'라고 했어요.

살리다 to save, to revive   만세 hurray   시간이 흐르다 time passes   따르다 to follow   신하 minister, servant, retainer   훔치다 to steal   못되다 to be evil, to be wicked   당장 at once   이곳저곳 here and there   번쩍하다 to appear and disappear quickly

"We are the Hwalbin gang! The name means we save the poor!"

"Hurrah for the Hwalbin gang!"

As time passed, the Hwalbin gang became famous, and more and more people started following Hong Gildong. This caught the attention of the king.

"What is the Hwalbin gang?"

The king asked his ministers. The yangbans who had become rich through bad means disliked the Hwalbin gang, so they lied.

"The Hwalbin gang consists of wicked thieves who steal from kindhearted people. We must capture them immediately."

After listening to his ministers, the king said, "Bring the Hwalbin gang to me at once! Especially their leader, Hong Gildong, you must capture him!"

When the ministers tried to capture Hong Gildong, he used magic and created seven fake Gildongs who looked exactly like him. With eight Gildongs appearing all over the place, the ministers could not catch Gildong. People did not know about the existence of the fake Gildongs, and when they saw Gildongs appearing here and there, they would say, "He flashes from the east, and he flashes from the west."

홍길동전

시간이 흐르자 사람들은 자신들을 도와준 홍길동을 잡지 말라고 외치기 시작했어요. 그러자
왕은 고민에 빠졌어요.
'이렇게 뛰어난 사람이라면 벌을 주지 않고, 오히려 나라를 위해 일하게 해야겠다.'
왕은 홍길동에게 벌을 주지 않고, 벼슬을 주겠다고 했어요. 그러자 며칠 후 홍길동이 스스로
왕을 찾아왔어요. 그리고 벼슬을 거절하며 말했어요.
"저는 벼슬이 없어도 됩니다. 대신 가난한 사람들을 위해 쌀과 돈을 나누어 주세요. 그러면 저는
조용히 떠나겠습니다."
왕은 그렇게 하겠다고 약속했어요.

이후 홍길동은 활빈당을 이끌고 바다를 건너 '율도'라는 섬으로 갔어요. 그리고 그곳에 양반과
노비가 없이 모두 똑같이 잘 사는 '율두국'이라는 나라를 세우고 행복하게 살았다고 해요.

외치다 to shout 벌 punishment 대신 instead 이끌다 to lead

일상 속에서 진짜 자주 등장하는 한국 옛날이야기

As time went on, people began voicing their desire for Hong Gildong to not be captured because he had helped them. This left the king in a dilemma.

"If he is such an exceptional person, I should not punish him, but rather make him work for the country."

The king said he would not punish Hong Gildong, but instead offer him a government position. A few days later, Hong Gildong went to the king himself and declined the offer, saying, "I do not need a government position. Rather, please distribute rice and money to the poor. Then I will leave quietly."

The king promised to do so.

After that, Hong Gildong led the Hwalbin gang and crossed the sea to an island called Yuldo. There, he established a country called "Yuldoguk" where everyone lived equally well, without yangbans or nobis, and they lived happily ever after.

Comprehension Quiz

Read the statements below and mark them as true or false.

1. 홍길동은 양반이 될 수 없었다. ———————————— True / False
2. 홍길동은 바위를 들어서 도적들의 대장이 되었다. ——————— True / False
3. 활빈당은 양반들을 살린다는 뜻이다. ———————————— True / False
4. 신하들은 홍길동을 잡았다. ———————————————— True / False
5. 홍길동은 율도국이라는 나라를 세웠다. ———————————— True / False

Modern Application

This story is possibly the most famous heroic novel in Korea that criticizes the social class system and corruption of its time. Because of its fame, when a virtual name is needed as an example, 홍길동 (Hong Gildong) is often used. In various official settings such as administrative offices, banks, and hospitals, where a sample form is provided to make it easy for people to fill out documents, you can often see 홍길동 in the name field. Even in non-official situations, you can use 홍길동 in need of anonymity, such as when you don't want to reveal your name when leaving a message with a gift for a friend.

In addition to the name Hong Gildong itself, there's a line from this novel that's also famous. "아버지를 아버지라고 부르지 못하고, 형을 형이라고 부르지 못한다. (= I can't call my father "father" or address my elder brother as "brother".)" is a frequently used quote, and the word 고 as in 라고 is usually dropped. This line is sometimes expressed briefly with Chinese characters as "호부호형하지 못한다." with the same meaning. It can also be used when you don't want to disclose a personal relationship in public, by replacing the word 아버지 or 형

with another title. For instance, when your mother is your teacher at school, it's better to avoid calling her 엄마 in front of your classmates. In such a case, you can jokingly say, " casual 엄마를 엄마라고 부르지도 못하고... (= I can't call my mom "mom"...)" You can also add 홍길동 too, like " casual 내가 무슨 홍길동이야? (= Am I Hong Gildong or something?)", " casual 내가 홍길동도 아니고. (= It's not like I'm Hong Gildong or anything.)", "저 완전 홍길동이에요. (= I'm totally Hong Gildong.)"

In the story, Hong Gildong appears in various places at the same time, and people described that situation as "동에서 번쩍하고 서에서 번쩍한다. (= He flashes from the east, and he flashes from the west.)" Therefore, the expression " casual '동에 번쩍, 서에 번쩍' 한다. (= Someone flashes from the east and the west.)" or " casual '동에 번쩍, 서에 번쩍'이다. (= It's like flashing from the east and the west.)" can be used to describe someone who is constantly moving around or very busy.

Example Dialogue (1)   Track 30

> (통화 중)
> 수호: 야, 나 지금 제주도 왔어.
> 다혜: 갑자기 제주도?
> 수호: 출장이 급하게 잡혔어. 내가 홍길동인 줄 아나 봐.
> 다혜: 그러니까 말야. 완전 '동에 번쩍, 서에 번쩍'이네.

> (On the phone)
> Suho: Hey, I just arrived on Jeju Island.
> Dahye: Jeju Island all of a sudden?

Suho: I got assigned on an urgent business trip. They must think I'm
       Hong Gildong.

Dahye: That's what I'm saying. You keep popping up everywhere.

Example Dialogue (2)

세아: 오예, 퇴근했다! 이제 자기라고 부를 수 있어. 자기야!

서준: 여자 친구를 여자 친구라 부르지 못하는 게 이렇게 힘들 줄이야.

세아: 그러니까, 무슨 홍길동 커플도 아니고. 그냥 확 말해 버릴까?

Se-ah: Yay, we're off work! Now I can call you "honey". Honey!

Seojun: I didn't know it would be this difficult to be unable to call
        my girlfriend "my girlfriend".

Se-ah: That's what I'm saying. We're not a Hong Gildong couple or
        something. Should we just tell them?

Answers

1. True 2. True 3. False 4. False 5. True

Grammar Point
Glossary

Grammar Point

01 I Am Not Scared of Tigers!

호랑이와 곶감 The Tiger and the Dried Persimmon

> ### -(으)ㄴ 줄 알다
>
> = to know/think that someone has done something; to know/think that something/someone is + descriptive verb
>
> It's used to express your knowledge or assumption about a past action or a present state. To make this expression a negative sentence, either change 알다 to 모르다, or add 안 to the verb that comes before -(으)ㄴ 줄 알다.
>
> Excerpt:
>
> 호랑이는 등에 곶감이라는 무서운 놈이 탄 줄 알고 힘껏 뛰기 시작했어요.
>
> The tiger, thinking that there was a scary dried persimmon on his back, started running with all its might.
>
> 호랑이도 곶감이 등에서 떨어진 줄 알고 더 빨리 뛰어 도망갔어요.
>
> The tiger also thought that the dried persimmon had fallen off its back and ran away faster.

02 Whatever You Say, I Will Do the Opposite

청개구리 이야기 The Green Frogs

> ### -(으)렴
>
> -(으)렴 is a casual language expression used for a gentle command or

일상 속에서 진짜 자주 등장하는 한국 옛날이야기

permission, which is why it's commonly used by parents or teachers toward young children. It can be used between close friends, too, but it's not typical in everyday usage.

Excerpt:

얘야, 더러운 곳에서 놀지 말렴.

Hey, do not play in dirty places.

내가 죽으면 나를 꼭 시냇가에 묻어 주렴.

When I die, make sure to bury me near the stream.

03 Darkness Cannot Stop Us
한석봉과 어머니 | Han Seokbong and His Mother

-아/어/여지다

It's used to express a change of state to mean "to become + descriptive verb".

Excerpt:

석봉의 친구들은 매일 밖에서 노는 것을 좋아했지만, 석봉은 친구들과 노는 것이 점점 지루해졌어요.

His friends liked to hang out outside every day, but he was gradually getting bored of hanging out with his friends.

글자를 쓸수록 공부하고 싶은 마음이 더 커졌어요.

The more he wrote letters, the more he wanted to study.

04 Magpies Never Forget

은혜 갚은 까치 | The Magpie Which Repaid a Favor

-(으)니

-(으)니 is attached to action verbs to explain what you discovered or what happened after the action. Since the following clause implies an event that already happened, it's mostly used in the past tense.

Excerpt:

남자가 까치 부부 쪽을 바라보니, 커다란 뱀이 까치 둥지로 슬금슬금 기어가고 있었어요.

When the man looked in the direction of the magpie couple, he saw a large snake slithering towards the magpie nest.

잘 곳이 있는지 주위를 둘러보니 저 멀리서 불빛이 보였어요.

When he looked around for a place to sleep, he saw a light in the distance.

남자가 불빛을 향해 다가가니 오래된 집이 하나 나타났어요.

As he approached the light, an old house appeared.

---

05 Or Else I Will Eat You

해와 달이 된 남매 | The Brother and Sister Who Became the Sun and the Moon

---

-(으)려고 하다

= to try to + action verb; to be planning to or to be about to + action verb

-(으)려고 하다 expresses the intention or will to do/want/try something. It's

---

also used when you talk about a plan or a state of something in the near future. For both usages, it's conjugated with action verbs.

Excerpt:

여동생이 문을 열려고 했어요.

The younger sister was going to open the door.

호랑이는 우물 안에 남매가 있는 줄 알고 우물에 들어가려고 했어요.

The tiger thought that the siblings were inside the well and tried to go into the well.

06 No Bottom, No Gain
콩쥐 팥쥐 | Kongjwi and Patjwi

-(으)시-

-(으)시- is an honorific ending used to show respect for the subject of the action or state. If the subject of a sentence is elderly or higher in the social hierarchy than you, or if you don't know that person very well, you can show respect by adding -(으)시- between the verb stem and the verb ending. This can be used to either the person whom you're directly talking to or someone else, but not to yourself.

There are some exceptions where this conjugation doesn't work, and the word itself is replaced with another word that implies respectfulness. Note that you should replace 먹다 with 드시다, 자다 with 주무시다, and 있다 with 계시다.

Excerpt:

원님 지나가신다!

Wonnim is passing by!

아까 부엌으로 간 아가씨도 불러 주시겠어요?

Would you please also call the girl who went to the kitchen earlier?

아가씨, 원님이 이 신발의 주인을 찾고 계십니다.

Miss, wonnim is looking for the owner of this shoe.

07 Uh-oh, This Is Unexpected
혹부리 할아버지 The Old Man with a Lump

-(는)구나

= I see that; I just realized that; I feel that

-(는)구나 is a casual language expression used to describe a newly found piece of information or situation. It can also be used when you're impressed or when you talk to yourself.
It's used in the form of -는구나 with action verbs and -구나 with descriptive verbs. If you want to use -(는)구나 in polite language, you can use -(는)군요. With nouns, you can simply add (이)구나 after a noun.

Excerpt:

얼씨구절씨구, 좋구나! 좋다!

Woohoo! That is good! It sounds nice!

이제 혹도 떼고, 큰 부자도 될 수 있겠구나!

Now I can get rid of my lump and become a wealthy man!

08 Making a Long Distance Relationship Work

견우와 직녀 Gyeonu and Jiknyeo

-게 되다

-게 되다 is usually attached to action verbs and used to express an outcome or a change of situation as a result of external influences. It's used when you didn't want, expect, or intend to do something, but you ended up doing it. However, it can also be used in a humble way to talk about the result that you intended. As it implies an outcome, it's common to use in the past tense like -게 되었어요/됐어요.

Excerpt:

그러던 어느 날, 직녀가 잠시 궁궐 밖으로 나갔다가 소를 몰고 있는 한 청년을 만나게 됐어요.

And then one day, while Jiknyeo was outside the palace, she met a young man herding cattle.

그렇게 견우와 직녀는 헤어지게 됐어요.

That is how Gyeonu and Jiknyeo had to part ways.

09 Confidence Maketh a Con Man

대동강을 판 김 선달 Seondal Kim Who Sold the Daedong River

-(으)ㄴ/는 대로

= in the way that; just like someone does; just like

It's used when an action is done exactly as described, requested or observed or the state of something remains exactly the same as it was before. It can be used after both action verbs and descriptive verbs, and it can also be used with nouns as "noun + 대로" to mean "just as", "in the way of", or "in accordance with".

Excerpt:

사람들은 김 선달과 약속한 대로 물을 풀 때마다 김 선달에게 동전을 냈어요.
As promised, people paid him coins every time they scooped water.

원하는 대로 돈을 드릴 수 있습니다.
We can give you as much as you want.

10 Don't Be Greedy, Bro!

흥부와 놀부 Heungbu and Nolbu

-아/어/여 보다

-아/어/여 보다 is attached to action verbs to mean "to try doing something". It can be used to say that you've done or tried something before, to ask if someone's ever done or tried something, to tell someone to try or attempt something, or to make a command sound less demanding.

Excerpt:

오늘은 형님 집에 찾아가 볼게요.

Today, I will visit my brother's house.

여보, 빨리 다른 박도 열어 봐요!

Honey, let us open the other gourds quickly!

11 How to Become an Actual Cow-boy

소가 된 게으름뱅이 The Lazy Man Who Became a Cow

-(았/었/였)던

-던 is used to recollect a past behavior or state attached to both descriptive verbs and action verbs. When you conjugate a descriptive verb with -던 before a noun, it means "a noun that was" or "a noun that used to be". -던 and -았/었/였던 are interchangeable, but -았/었/였던 is more frequently used. When an action verb is used with -던, it implies an action hasn't finished or an action was repeated in the past. In contrast, When an action verb is used with -았/었/였던, it means an action's been completed and didn't continue.

Excerpt:

부인의 잔소리가 듣기 싫었던 게으름뱅이는 집을 나갔어요.

He left home because he did not want to hear his wife's nagging.

집을 나간 게으름뱅이는 그늘에서 풀을 뜯어 먹고 있던 소를 보고 말했어요.

After he left home, the lazy man saw a cow grazing in the shade and said,

그때 마침 게으름뱅이 앞을 지나가던 노인이 게으름뱅이에게 말을 걸었어요.

Just at that moment, an old man was passing in front of him and talked to him.

12 Doppelganger Alert

손톱 먹은 쥐 The Mouse That Ate Fingernails

-아/어/여라

It's used for an assertive command or a strong request to somebody younger or lower in social status, conjugated with action verbs. -아/어/여라 is considered more formal and forceful than -아/어/여, so make sure not to use it when speaking to someone who's older than you, no matter how close you are.

Excerpt:

손톱을 잘 모아서 버린 다음, 얼른 가서 자라.

After gathering the trimmed nails properly and throwing them away, hurry up and go get some sleep.

부모님의 생신이 언제인지 말해 봐라.

Tell me when your parents' birthdays are.

가짜 아들에게 벌을 주어라!

Punish the fake son!

13　A Huge Fan of Garlic

단군 이야기 | The Dan-gun Story

-(으)면서

It's used when you're engaging in two actions at the same time or when something maintains two states at the same time, added at the end of verbs. You can use this structure with nouns, too, in which case the structure changes to "noun + -(이)면서".

Excerpt:

호랑이와 곰의 간절한 부탁에 환웅은 쑥과 마늘을 주면서 말했어요.

Since the tiger and the bear made their request earnestly, Hwanung handed them mugwort and garlic and said,

사람이 되려면 100일 동안 햇빛을 보지 않고, 이 쑥과 마늘만 먹으면서 지내야 한다.

To become human, you must live for 100 days without seeing sunlight, only eating mugwort and garlic.

14　Someone Is in My House!

우렁이 각시 | The Snail Bride

-(ㄴ/는)다

It's a narrative present tense form used when you're talking or writing about life events. You can use -(ㄴ/는)다 when you want to show your reaction or impression when talking about a present action or situation. When using -(ㄴ/는)다 in speaking, you can only use it to someone who isn't older than you, who is at a lower social status than yours, or with whom you're close.

In writing, on the contrary, it's not intended for any specific audience and used to describe the events or situation objectively. Thus, it's commonly used wherever a neutral and narrative voice is required such as in articles, documents, books, documentary films, recipes, or personal journals.

Excerpt:

이 여인은 나와 사는 것이 좋겠다!

It would be better if this woman lived with me!

내가 졌다.

I lost.

15 The Most Famous Name in Korea
홍길동전 The Tale of Hong Gildong

-(이)라는

-(이)라는 is a shortened form of -(이)라고 하는 which means "a noun + that is called + a noun". You can use this when you want to introduce what something is called or how it's described. It's sometimes used to talk about an abstract concept and its innate characteristics philosophically.

Excerpt:

조선 시대에 홍길동이라는 남자아이가 살고 있었어요.

In the Joseon Dynasty, there lived a boy named Hong Gildong.

일상 속에서 진짜 자주 등장하는 한국 옛날이야기

이후 홍길동은 활빈당을 이끌고 바다를 건너 '율도'라는 섬으로 갔어요.

After that, Hong Gildong led the Hwalbin gang and crossed the sea to an island called Yuldo.

Glossary

01 I Am Not Scared of Tigers!

호랑이와 곶감 The Tiger and the Dried
Persimmon

곶감	dried persimmon
어흥	roar
배고프다	to be hungry
울음소리	crying sound
으앙	waaah (sound of a baby crying)
소리가 나다	to sound
오호	aha
다가가다	to approach
여전히	still
얘	hey, kid
도깨비	goblin
잡아가다	to take away
울음	crying
그치다	to stop
당황하다	to be puzzled
곧바로	immediately
놈	disapproving/casual guy
외양간	barn
도망가다	to run away
살금살금	quietly
훔치다	to steal
소도둑	cattle thief
벌벌	mimetic word describing someone trembling
떨다	to tremble
엎드리다	to lie face down
숨다	to hide
다가오다	to approach, to come toward
더듬다	to fumble
벌떡	mimetic word describing someone standing up suddenly
올라타다	to get onto
아이고	jeez
힘껏	with all one's might
매달리다	to hang onto, to cling onto
어느새	before one knows
그제야	only then
세상에	oh my
커다랗다	to be big
재빨리	quickly
피하다	to avoid
잡아먹다	to feed on, to prey on

02 Whatever You Say, I Will Do the Opposite

청개구리 이야기 The Green Frogs

청개구리	tree frog, green frog
연못	pond
말을 듣다	to do as one is told
거꾸로	in reverse
얘	hey, kid
지저분하다	to be dirty
흙탕물	muddy water
마구	wildly, carelessly
헤엄치다	to swim

숲속	forest		떡	rice cake
뱀	snake		글자	letter
일부러	deliberately		지루하다	to be boring/bored
하마터면	almost		서당	elementary school during the Joseon Dynasty
잡아먹다	to feed on, to prey on		가난하다	to be poor
개굴개굴	rib-bit, rib-bit (sound that a frog makes)		글씨	handwriting, calligraphy
무조건	unconditionally, definitely		화가	painter
속상하다	to be upset		종이	paper
어휴	sound of sighing		실망하다	to be disappointed
병에 걸리다	to fall ill		나뭇가지	tree branch
시냇가	stream bank, by the stream		따라 쓰다	to trace (letters), to copy (words)
묻다	to bury		붓	brush
절대	never		와	wow
세상을 떠나다	to die, to pass away		흐뭇하다	to be pleased
눈물을 흘리다	to shed tears		제대로	properly
펑펑	mimetic word describing a large amount of liquid pouring at once		한양	*Hanyang*, the name of Seoul during the Joseon Dynasty
돌아가시다	to pass away		각오	determination
흑흑	sound of sobbing		단호하다	to be adamant, to be firm
후회하다	to regret		무척	very
무덤	grave		집중하다	to concentrate
떠내려가다	to be washed away		고생하다	to go through a hardship
정말로	really		도대체	(who/what/where) on earth
			꾹	mimetic word describing the action of holding back or pressing something hard

03 Darkness Cannot Stop Us

한석봉과 어머니 Han Seokbong and His Mother

돌아가시다	to pass away		반기다	to welcome
			당황하다	to be puzzled
			실력	skills, ability

정말로	really	과거 시험	the national civil service examinations under the Goryeo and Joseon Dynasties
완벽하다	to be perfect	날아오다	to fly over here
자신이 없다	to be not confident	커다랗다	to be large
삐뚤빼뚤	uneven	뱀	snake
엉망	mess	둥지	nest
두께	thickness	슬금슬금	stealthily, slowly
모양	shape	기어가다	to crawl
명필	masterful calligraphy, master calligrapher	겁에 질리다	to be in fear
눈물을 흘리다	to shed tears	서두르다	to rush
자만하다	to be conceited	한참	a long while
매달리다	to be preoccupied with	구하다	to save
최선을 다하다	to do one's best	둘러보다	to look around
조선	*Joseon*, the name of Korea from 1392 to 1910	불빛	light
소문	rumor	향하다	to face
마침내	finally	다가가다	to approach, to go toward
꼭	tightly, firmly, exactly, definitely	두드리다	to knock
장하다	to be admirable	저녁밥	dinner
껴안다	to hug	차리다	to set (the table)
		잠이 들다	to fall asleep
		숨이 막히다	to suffocate

04 Magpies Never Forget

은혜 갚은 까치 | The Magpie Which Repaid a Favor

은혜를 갚다	to repay a favor	감다	to wind, to twine
까치	magpie	복수하다	to avenge, to get one's revenge
활	bow	변신하다	to transform
쏘다	to shoot	간절히	sincerely
한양	*Hanyang*, the name of Seoul during the Joseon Dynasty	잡아먹다	to feed on, to prey on
		가만히	doing nothing, staying still
		용서하다	to forgive

절	temple	막다	to stop
종	bell	당황하다	to be flustered
울리다	to ring	쉬다	to be hoarse
눈물을 흘리다	to shed tears	내밀다	to stick out, to reach out
종소리	sound of a bell	문틈	a crevice or gap in the door
들려오다	to sound, to reach one's ears	거칠다	to be rough
댕	dong, sound of a large bell ringing	털	fur
또다시	once again	엿보다	to peek
산꼭대기	mountaintop	세상에	oh my
발견하다	to find	도망가다	to run away
부딪치다	to crash	문밖	outside the door
묻다	to bury	뒷문	back door
		통하다	to pass through
		뒷마당	backyard

05 Or Else I Will Eat You

해와 달이 된 남매 The Brother and Sister Who Became the Sun and the Moon

남매	brother and sister, son and daughter	뒤늦다	to be late
		발견하다	to find
산골	mountain, mountain valley	우물	well
떡	rice cake	비치다	to be reflected
밤늦다	to be late at night	나뭇잎	leaf
커다랗다	to be big	사라지다	to disappear
어흥	roar	따르다	to follow
잡아먹다	to feed on, to prey on	가까워지다	to get closer
얼른	quickly	꼭	tightly
한입	one bite	기도하다	to pray
살리다	to spare one's life	기적	miracle
두드리다	to knock	동아줄	rope
		쑥	mimetic word describing something going up/down suddenly

매달리다	to grab onto	발견하다	to discover
데리다	to take/bring someone	못되다	to be mean
뚝	mimetic word describing something hard being broken or snapped	앗	oh
		흑흑	sound of sobbing
끊어지다	to snap	속상하다	to be upset
으악	sound of screaming	두꺼비	toad
썩다	to rot, to be rotten	얼른	quickly
못되다	to be mean	잔치	feast
무사히	safely	어울리다	to suit
비추다	to shine	벼	rice
		껍질	husk
		벗기나	to peel off

06 No Bottom, No Gain

콩쥐 | 팥쥐 | Kongjwi and Patjwi

여자아이	girl, baby girl
돌아가시다	to pass away
새어머니	stepmother
사이좋다	to be on good terms
맞다	to welcome, to greet, to fit
집안일	household chores
항아리	traditional Korean earthenware jar
채우다	to fill
얘	hey, kid
저녁때	evening
저녁밥	dinner
붓다	to pour
살펴보다	to examine
구멍	hole

베	hemp cloth
짜다	to weave
휴	phew
참새	sparrow
선녀	fairy in Korean fairy tales, usually wearing a dress
원님	⌜honorific⌝ *wonnim*, term used to address a local governor in the Joseon Dynasty
비키다	to make way
강물	river water
첫눈에 반하다	to fall in love at first sight
당황하다	to be flustered
사라지다	to vanish
신하	servant, retainer, subject
돌아다니다	to go around

어허	sound that people make when they are displeased with someone who is younger or in a lower societal position
마음에 들다	to like
사랑에 빠지다	to fall in love

07 Uh-oh, This Is Unexpected
혹부리 할아버지 The Old Man with a Lump

혹부리	playful nickname for a person with a lump on one's face
턱	chin, jaw
혹	lump
달리다	to hang
마음씨	attitude, heart
구하다	to find, to look for
빗방울	raindrop
둘러보다	to look around
허름하다	to be shabby
하룻밤	one night
얼씨구절씨구	sympathetic response people make when cheering to Korean traditional music
생기다	to look
도깨비	goblin
표정	facial expression
차분하다	to be calm
정신을 차리다	to collect one's mind
무사히	safely

내놓다	to put
대신	in return, instead
보물	treasure
도깨비방망이	goblin's magic club
툭	sound of hitting something lightly
떼다	to take something off
온갖	all kinds of
잔뜩	a lot
욕심	greed
욕심쟁이	disapproving/casual greedy person
당장	right away, immediately
깜깜하다	to be very dark
신나다	to be excited
노랫소리	singing voice
거짓말쟁이	liar
가짜	fake
속다	to be fooled
당황하다	to be flustered
이놈	brat
욕심을 부리다	to be greedy

08 Making a Long Distance Relationship Work
견우와 직녀 Gyeonu and Jiknyeo

임금님	king
마음씨	attitude, heart
베	hemp cloth
짜다	to weave

옷감	cloth
반짝반짝	mimetic word describing something shining
빛이 나다	to shine
어쩜	how
궁궐	palace
몰다	to herd
청년	young man
농부	farmer
순간	moment
사랑에 빠지다	to fall in love
허락하다	to allow
혼을 내다	to scold
용서하다	to forgive
돌보다	to take care of
결국	eventually
도저히	(cannot) possibly
당장	immediately
은하수	the Milky Way
벌을 내리다	to punish
눈물을 흘리다	to shed tears
사이에 두다	to put something in between
마침내	finally
달려가다	to run
펑펑	mimetic word describing a large amount of liquid pouring at once
홍수가 나다	to flood
날아다니다	to fly around
까마귀	crow

까치	magpie
잇다	to connect
밟다	to step on
조심스럽다	to be careful
밤하늘	night sky

09 Confidence Maketh a Con Man

대동강을 판 김 선달 Seondal Kim Who Sold the Daedong River

대동강	*the Daedong River*, the name of a large river in North Korea
선달	*seondal*, person who passed the civil service examination but does not have a government position yet under the Joseon Dynasty
속이다	to trick
한양	*Hanyang*, the name of Seoul during the Joseon Dynasty
상인	merchant
얄밉다	to be unlikable or annoying because one is too smart or cunning
골탕 먹이다	to put someone through trouble
푸다	to scoop
눈빛	eyes, look in one's eyes
반짝이다	to sparkle
어리둥절하다	to be puzzled
표정을 짓다	to make a (certain) look
마침	just, just in time
심지어	even

내내	throughout		짓다	to build
마르다	to dry, to go dry		구하다	to find
합치다	to combine		배고프다	to be hungry
결심하다	to decide, to make up one's mind		여보	honey (to one's wife or husband)
다가가다	to approach		형님	honorific older brother
함부로	indiscreetly		굶다	to starve
돌아가시다	to pass away		이놈	brat
얼른	quickly		빗자루	broom
큰돈	a lot of money		달려가다	to run
상관없다	to not care, to not matter		때리다	to hit
적어도	at least		주걱	(rice) paddle
십만	a hundred thousand		뺨	cheek
어이없다	to be dumbfounded		찰싹	sound of a slap
그제야	only after, only then		밥알	grain of cooked rice
도망가다	to run away		달라붙다	to stick
사기꾼	swindler		내밀다	to stick out
			형수	one's elder brother's wife
			당장	right now

10 Don't Be Greedy, Bro!

흥부와 놀부 Heungbu and Nolbu

욕심	greed
돌아가시다	to pass away
사이좋다	to be on good terms
재산	property, wealth
욕심쟁이	disapproving/casual greedy person
차지하다	to possess, to take
내쫓다	to kick out
오두막집	shack

결국	in the end
시간이 흐르다	time passes
제비	swallow
쌍	pair
지붕	roof
둥지	nest
알	egg
빙글빙글	round and round, in circles
물다	to have something in one's mouth
툭	sound of something dropping

떨어뜨리다	to drop
박씨	gourd seed
커다랗다	to be big
박	gourd
주렁주렁	mimetic word describing fruits hanging in clusters
열리다	(fruit) to appear/grow (on the tree)
따다	to pick
펑	bang
갈라지다	to split
쏟아져 나오다	to pour out
웬	what, why
얼른	quickly
보물	treasure
세상에	oh my
그다음	the next
수많다	to be numerous
하인	servant
질투가 나다	to be jealous
찾아다니다	to go in search for
마침	just, just in time
발견하다	to find
일부러	purposely
부러뜨리다	to break
흐흐	sound of laughing wickedly or cunningly
정말로	really
신이 나다	to be excited
도깨비	goblin

못되다	to be mean
혼내다	to scold
부수다	to destroy
거지	beggar
흑흑	sound of sobbing
벌	punishment
반성하다	to reflect on
달려오다	to come running
진심	one's heart, one's true feelings
사과하다	to apologize
용서하다	to forgive
데리다	to take/bring someone
오순도순	mimetic word describing people getting along well with each other

11 **How to Become an Actual Cow-boy**

소가 된 게으름뱅이 The Lazy Man Who Became a Cow

게으름뱅이	disapproving/casual	lazy person
종일	all day	
한심하다	to be pathetic	
여보	honey (to one's wife or husband)	
당신	honey (to one's wife or husband)	
먹고살다	to make a living	
잔소리	nagging	
그늘	shade	
풀	grass	
뜯다	to pluck	

마침	just, just in time
탈	mask
얼른	immediately
펑	pop
와	wow
신나다	to be excited
건네주다	to hand over
끌다	to drag
이랴	giddy up
이놈	rascal
소리치다	to exclaim, to shout
음메	moo
울음소리	crying sound
농부	farmer
넘기다	to hand over
절대	never
참	very
여전히	still
밭	field
게으름을 피우다	to be lazy
벌	punishment
아이고	jeez
지난날	the past days
후회하다	to regret
반성하다	to reflect on (in self-examination)
무밭	radish field
차라리	rather
신기하다	to be marvellous

벌어지다	to happen

12 Doppelganger Alert

손톱 먹은 쥐 The Mouse That Ate Fingernails

손톱	fingernail
쥐	mouse
어휴	sound of sighing
종일	all day
절	temple
스님	honorific Buddhist monk
엄격하다	to be strict
오	oh
놀고먹다	to live idle, to do nothing but play and eat
당장	right now
억지로	forcefully
허름하다	to be shabby
아이고	jeez
한숨을 쉬다	to sigh
다가오다	to approach, to come toward
얼른	quickly
휙	quickly
이놈	rascal
함부로	carelessly
큰일	big trouble
달라지다	to change
찍찍	squeak
가만히	motionlessly

신기하다	to find something intriguing	흑흑	sound of sobbing
알아듣다	to understand	떠오르다	to strike, to occur to
애	hey, kid	눈물을 흘리다	to shed tears
예전	the past	숨기다	to hide
어느덧	before one knows	내쫓다	to kick out
흐르다	to flow, to pass	달려가다	to run
와	wow	펑	pop
신나다	to be excited	그러게	I told you so
에잇	sound that someone makes when they knowingly make a careless decision	반성하다	to reflect on (in self-examination)
		게으름을 피우다	to be lazy
향하다	to face		
결국	eventually		
뛰어나오다	to rush out	**13 A Huge Fan of Garlic**	
세상에	oh my	단군 이야기 The Dan-gun Story	
번갈아	in turn, back and forth		
심지어	even	임금님	[honorific] king
점	dot, mole	인간	human
데리다	to take/bring someone	지켜보다	to observe
원님	[honorific] *wonnim*, term used to address a local governor in the Joseon Dynasty	방울	bell
		섬기다	to serve (king, god)
		신하	servant, retainer, subject
당황하다	to be flustered	다스리다	to govern, to rule
더듬거리다	to stutter	소원	wish
재빨리	quickly	들어주다	to grant (one's wish)
벌	punishment	간절하다	to be earnest
매	rod	쑥	mugwort
맞다	to be hit, to be beaten	마늘	garlic
쫓겨나다	to be kicked out	깜깜하다	to be very dark
후회하다	to regret	동굴	cave

고통스럽다	to be agonizing		각시	bride, wife
에잇	sound that someone makes when they knowingly make a careless decision		성실하다	to be diligent
			논	rice paddy, field
당장	right now		혼잣말	talking to oneself
달래다	to calm, to comfort		어휴	sound of sighing
견디다	to endure		주변	surroundings
뛰쳐나가다	to dash out		둘러보다	to look around
환하다	to be bright		커다랗다	to be large
대견하다	to be proud		신기하다	to find something intriguing
세상에	oh my		항아리	traditional Korean earthenware jar
정말로	truly		알아내다	to find out
감격하다	to be deeply moved		숨다	to hide
기도하다	to pray		지켜보다	to observe
흑흑	sound of sobbing		첫눈에 반하다	to fall in love at first sight
정성	devotion, one's heart		얼른	quickly
감동하다	to be touched		당신	honorific you
시간이 흐르다	time passes		용왕	the Dragon King
우렁차다	to be loud and powerful		벌	punishment
아가	word used to address a baby		감동하다	to be touched
훗날	some day		함께하다	to be with
바람	wish		진심	one's heart, one's true feelings
최초	the first		하루하루	every day, from day to day
고조선	*Gojoseon*, the name of the first nation of Korea		못되다	to be mean
			소문나다	a rumor circulates, to be talked about

14 Someone Is in My House!

우렁이 각시 | The Snail Bride

우렁이	freshwater snail

원님	honorific *wonnim*, term used to address a local governor in the Joseon Dynasty
여인	woman
가난하다	to be poor

내기	bet	무술	martial arts
뒷산	mountain behind one's house or town	벼슬	government position
큰돈	large sum of money	양반	*yangban*, gentry of dynastic Korea during the Goryeo and Joseon Dynasties
억울하다	to feel wronged		
피하다	to avoid	노비	*nobi*, slave class during the Goryeo and Joseon Dynasties
흑흑	sound of sobbing		
건네주다	to hand over	인정	acknowledgment, recognition
절대로	never	갑갑하다	to feel frustrated
곧바로	immediately	위로하다	to comfort
벌어지다	to happen	자만하다	to be big-headed, to be conceited
바닷속	under the sea	일부러	purposely
신하	servant, retainer, subject	엄하다	to be strict, to be harsh
포기하다	to give up	진심	one's heart, one's true feelings
아이고	jeez	속상하다	to be upset
결국	in the end	재빨리	quickly
초라하다	to be shabby, to be humble	공격하다	to attack
파도	wave	빼앗다	to take, to extort
치다	(wave) to crash	산속	inside the mountains
뒤집다	to overturn	도적	thief
		대장	leader
		바위	rock

15 The Most Famous Name in Korea

홍길동전 The Tale of Hong Gildong

-전	biography, life (story)	당당하다	to be confident
조선 시대	*Joseon Dynasty*, the name of the last dynastic kingdom of Korea (1392-1910)	무시하다	to look down on
		하하	haha
		번쩍	lightly, effortlessly
남자아이	boy	괴롭히다	to torment
		가난하다	to be poor
		혼내다	to scold
		지혜롭다	to be wise

능력	ability
뛰어나다	to be exceptional
살리다	to save, to revive
만세	hurray
시간이 흐르다	time passes
따르다	to follow
신하	minister, servant, retainer
훔치다	to steal
못되다	to be evil, to be wicked
당장	at once
이곳저곳	here and there
번쩍하다	to appear and disappear quickly
외치다	to shout
벌	punishment
대신	instead
이끌다	to lead

TTMIK Book Audio App

Download our app TTMIK: Audio to listen to all the audio and video tracks from our book conveniently on your phone! The app is available for free on both iOS and Android. Search for TTMIK: Audio in your app store.